FEDERALISM AND DEMOCRACY IN BRAZIL AND BEYOND

Editora Appris Ltda.
1.ª Edição - Copyright© 2024 dos autores
Direitos de Edição Reservados à Editora Appris Ltda.

Nenhuma parte desta obra poderá ser utilizada indevidamente, sem estar de acordo com a Lei nº 9.610/98. Se incorreções forem encontradas, serão de exclusiva responsabilidade de seus organizadores. Foi realizado o Depósito Legal na Fundação Biblioteca Nacional, de acordo com as Leis nos 10.994, de 14/12/2004, e 12.192, de 14/01/2010.

Catalogação na Fonte
Elaborado por: Dayanne Leal Souza
Bibliotecária CRB 9/2162

F293f 2024	Federalism and democracy in Brazil and beyond / Eduardo Grin, Rogerio Schlegel e Johanna Schnabel (eds.). – 1. ed. – Curitiba: Appris, 2024. 204 p. : il. ; 23 cm.
	Inclui referências. Vários autores. ISBN 978-65-250-6294-5
	1. Federalism. 2. Democracy. 3. Intergovernmental relations. I. Grin, Eduardo. II. Schlegel, Rogerio. III. Schnabel, Johanna. IV. Título. V. Série.
	CDD – 321.8

Livro de acordo com a normalização técnica da APA

Appris
editora

Editora e Livraria Appris Ltda.
Av. Manoel Ribas, 2265 – Mercês
Curitiba/PR – CEP: 80810-002
Tel. (41) 3156-4731
www.editoraappris.com.br

Printed in Brazil
Impresso no Brasil

Eduardo Grin
Rogerio Schlegel
Johanna Schnabel

(eds.)

With the assistance of Camila Nastari Fernandes

FEDERALISM AND DEMOCRACY IN BRAZIL AND BEYOND

Appris editora

Curitiba, PR

2024

FICHA TÉCNICA

EDITORIAL	Augusto Coelho
	Sara C. de Andrade Coelho
COMITÊ EDITORIAL	Ana El Achkar (Universo/RJ)
	Andréa Barbosa Gouveia (UFPR)
	Antonio Evangelista de Souza Netto (PUC-SP)
	Belinda Cunha (UFPB)
	Délton Winter de Carvalho (FMP)
	Edson da Silva (UFVJM)
	Eliete Correia dos Santos (UEPB)
	Erineu Foerste (UFES)
	Erineu Foerste (Ufes)
	Fabiano Santos (UERJ-IESP)
	Francinete Fernandes de Sousa (UEPB)
	Francisco Carlos Duarte (PUCPR)
	Francisco de Assis (Fiam-Faam-SP-Brasil)
	Gláucia Figueiredo (UNIPAMPA/ UDELAR)
	Jacques de Lima Ferreira (UNOESC)
	Jean Carlos Gonçalves (UFPR)
	José Wálter Nunes (UnB)
	Junia de Vilhena (PUC-RIO)
	Lucas Mesquita (UNILA)
	Márcia Gonçalves (Unitau)
	Maria Aparecida Barbosa (USP)
	Maria Margarida de Andrade (Umack)
	Marilda A. Behrens (PUCPR)
	Marília Andrade Torales Campos (UFPR)
	Marli Caetano
	Patrícia L. Torres (PUCPR)
	Paula Costa Mosca Macedo (UNIFESP)
	Ramon Blanco (UNILA)
	Roberta Ecleide Kelly (NEPE)
	Roque Ismael da Costa Güllich (UFFS)
	Sergio Gomes (UFRJ)
	Tiago Gagliano Pinto Alberto (PUCPR)
	Toni Reis (UP)
	Valdomiro de Oliveira (UFPR)
SUPERVISOR DA PRODUÇÃO	Renata Cristina Lopes Miccelli
PRODUÇÃO EDITORIAL	Sabrina Costa
REVISÃO	Jose A Ramos Junior
DIAGRAMAÇÃO	Andrezza Libel
CAPA	Eneo Lage
REVISÃO DE PROVA	Sabrina Costa

TABLE OF CONTENTS

INTRODUCTION 9
Eduardo Grin
Rogerio Schlegel
Johanna Schnabel

1
NEW DIRECTIONS IN THE PRACTICE OF FEDERALISM – THE ROLE OF THE FORUM OF FEDERATIONS 23
Rupak Chattopadhyay

2
FEDERALISM AND FEDERATIONS: AN INTRODUCTORY OVERVIEW ... 29
Alan Fenna

3
FEDERALISM AND FEDERATIONS: THE BRAZILIAN PERSPECTIVE .. 45
Marta Arretche

4
FEDERALISM, POLITICS IN TIME, AND THE WELFARE STATE AS A CRISIS MANAGER IN THE UNITED STATES AND CANADA 53
Daniel Béland

5
FEDERALISM AND DEMOCRACY: CONNECTIONS AND CHALLENGES .. 63
Jared Sonnicksen

6
FEDERALISM AND DEMOCRACY IN CONTEMPORARY FEDERALISM: OVERCOMING A LONG TRAJECTORY OF DECOUPLING AND CREATING NEW FORMS OF COUPLING 73
Fernando Luiz Abrucio

7
LOCAL GOVERNMENTS AS LABORATORIES OF DEMOCRATIC INNOVATIONS? THE ROLE OF NATIONAL COORDINATION AND INTERGOVERNMENTAL RELATIONS IN BRAZIL........................ 87
Catarina Ianni Segatto

8
FEDERALISM AND TERRITORIAL RESPONSES TO DIVERSITY IN AFRICA AND THEIR IMPLICATIONS.. 97
Zemelak Ayitenew Ayele

9
IS DIVERSITY TURNING INTO DISUNITY IN BRAZIL?................. 113
Rogerio Schlegel

10
FEDERALISM AND RECENTRALIZATION: NEW TREND IN INTERGOVERNMENTAL RELATIONS? AN ACCOUNT FROM MEXICO.. 123
Juan C. Olmeda

11
THE DILIGENCE AND RESILIENCE OF RECENTRALIZATION REFORMS IN BRAZIL... 133
Daniel Arias Vazquez

12
MANAGING INTERDEPENDENCIES IN FEDERAL SYSTEMS.......... 143
Johanna Schnabel

13
MANAGING INTERGOVERNMENTAL RELATIONS IN BRAZIL: TYPES, STRUCTURES, AND FUNCTIONING.. 157
Eduardo Grin

14
NEW PATHS FOR BRAZILIAN FEDERALISM: THE CREATION OF THE COUNCIL OF THE FEDERATION 169
André Luis Nogueira da Silva
Elaine Cristina Lício

15
THE ROLE OF SECOND CHAMBERS IN FEDERATIONS: A COMPARATIVE APPROACH 179
Antonios Souris

16
THE ROLE OF UPPER HOUSES IN FEDERATIONS: THE BRAZILIAN PERSPECTIVE 189
Cláudio Gonçalves Couto

ABOUT THE EDITORS 197

ABOUT THE ASSISTANT EDITOR 199

ABOUT THE AUTHORS 201

INTRODUCTION

Eduardo Grin
Rogerio Schlegel
Johanna Schnabel

The book **Federalism and Democracy in Brazil and Beyond** is the result of the seminar on "Federalism in an Era of Emergencies", which was held in July 2023 at Fundação Getulio Vargas of São Paulo. The seminar was organized by Fundação Getulio Vargas of São Paulo, The Federal University of São Paulo, and Freie Universität Berlin. The event also received support from the Forum of Federations, the São Paulo Research Foundation (Fapesp)[1], FGV Research, and the Council of Federation, launched in 2023 by the Brazilian government. It brought together international and Brazilian academics, as well as practitioners. The seminar reflected on federalism in a post-COVID-19 scenario, during which countries organized by this form of territorial division of power experimented with different models of confronting and managing the pandemic. Different instruments were employed for intergovernmental cooperation and steered by national governments. The pandemic highlighted the importance of federalism, which was a core motivation for organizing the seminar.

Challenges such as climate emergency and democratic backsliding represent contemporary contexts that take on particular contours in federal, quasi-federal, and decentralized countries. This includes the need to coordinate public policies across different spheres of government (Arretche, 2012; Schnabel, 2020), the potential of subnational governments to serve as innovation laboratories, and the importance of (re)distributing resources, tax authority, and policy responsibilities vertically and horizontally in the best possible way (Fenna, 2022). At the same time, issues related to democratic legitimacy take on even more complex contours in these countries, due to different territorial allegiances and the challenge of party and electoral systems that tend to be more pluralistic and multifaceted than those found in unitary countries.

Recent years have provided valuable insights into the potential and limitations of multilevel governance and federal arrangements in addressing

---

[1] Grant numbers 2021/08773-5 and 2023/05568-7.

challenges such as the COVID-19 pandemic (Peters, Grin, & Abrucio, 2021; Vazquez & Schlegel, 2022). While the acute phase of the COVID-19 pandemic has passed, other equally daunting crises remain possible. The climate emergency continues to deepen alongside threats to democracy in various countries. Growing polarization makes immigration and ethnicity contentious topics in increasingly divided polities. Federalism and federal countries occupy a central position in these debates due to their territorial division of power.

Populist presidents in federal countries – such as Bolsonaro and Trump – seek to undermine federal coordination and cooperation to centralize decision-making in areas where the constitutional pact assigns responsibilities to each sphere of government (Peters et al., 2021). Such political actions can weaken, undermine, and ultimately eliminate institutionalized arenas of federal safeguards and intergovernmental relations. This also represents a dimension of democratic backsliding as it can affect the vertical division of powers as well as the autonomy of directly elected local authorities.

Yet, federalism can also contain democratic backsliding since the division of powers between different orders of government creates constitutional and political obstacles for populist and authoritarian presidents to encroach on the autonomy of constituent units. This was the case of the Brazilian federation under Bolsonaro's presidency. States and municipalities were resilient against the centralization proposed by the federal government, especially during the COVID-19 pandemic (Abrucio et al., 2020). As states and municipalities elect their own authorities, governors and mayors were first and foremost accountable to their constituencies. Democratic backsliding is a reality in some federations (for example, Mexico and India), threatened other federations in recent years (for example, Brazil and the USA) and recently happened in Argentina. In fact, there is nothing to indicate that federal countries will no longer face challenges in maintaining and strengthening democracy as a political regime.

Against this backdrop, this book aims to build knowledge on issues of global relevance in the field of comparative federalism. In line with the international seminar in São Paulo, our approach addresses these topics and the position of Brazilian federalism in this debate. This book aims to build knowledge on issues of global relevance in the field of comparative federalism. The title of the book summarizes these two objectives, and, for this reason, the chapters are organized to provide an introduction to the central themes of federalism and their current application to the Brazilian context. The book encompasses the four underlying axes discussed at the seminar. Firstly, one axis on institutional design, structuring, functioning and perspectives of federalism. Secondly, a reflection on federalism and democracy, which also includes the debate on democratic innovations regarding society's participation. Thirdly, a topic on de/re/centralization in federations. Finally, an axis on federalism and public health policies. As the authors offer rather intertwined discussions of these topics, we opted not to compartmentalize the chapters in discrete blocks.

The relevance of studying federalism in an era of emergencies

The complexity of contemporary societies, the expansion of integration between countries and the reduction of territorial barriers as well as the expansion of the welfare state have influenced the growing state intervention in many public policies, especially from the second half of the 20th century onwards (Obinger, Leibfried, & Castels, 2005). In this context, how federations address problems that affect all orders of government is of great importance (Loughlin, Kincaid, & Sweden, 2013). In federal countries, due to the existence of autonomous levels of government that formulate and implement public policies, intergovernmental coordination is one of the most challenging issues.

In times of growing crises and emergencies, federations are confronted with complex intergovernmental problems (Paquet & Schertzer, 2020). Intergovernmental coordination can be challenging, but the absence of shared solutions can generate high social costs, as seen during the COVID-19 pandemic in federations where intergovernmental collaboration was weak or non-existent.

According to the Chattopadhyay's chapter in this book, many threats and new trends such as Artificial Intelligence, digitalization, recessions, global slowdowns, inflation and growing cost of living are likely to increase social discontent, which undermines and challenges democratic systems of governance. In federal countries, managing them also requires effective intergovernmental coordination and careful balancing of roles and responsibilities of different governments.

There is no evidence suggesting that federalism is generally more effective or less able to address emergencies such as pandemics, financial crises, and climate change. On the one hand, federalism allows to tailor measures to local circumstances and needs. It creates additional checks and balances and promotes negotiation and dialogue, forcing governments to justify their decisions. Federalism furthermore can encourage competition for best solutions and policy learning; contain government overreach and policy failures; avoid blanket approaches; and offer political alternatives. All this can enhance the quality of crisis management. On the other hand, federalism can lead to a patchwork of measures, slow responses, intergovernmental conflict and blame games, inconsistency leadership, competition for resources, and containment of best practices. How these trade-offs play out differs between dual and administrative federations, centralized and decentralized federal states, and those with strong and weak intergovernmental mechanisms (Hegele & Schnabel, 2021). Outcomes are also contingent on other factors, such as the severity of the crisis and crisis preparedness, as well as political culture and leadership.

Pandemics, other health crises, climate change, and immigration issues are expected to be more frequent and conspicuous in the near future. These different crises cross geographical, political, and administrative borders, and test the organizational capacity of states to cope with them. As federations are characterized by a division of powers between at least two orders of government, these countries will need to develop or improve their instruments to deal with these challenges.

1. Federalism: institutional design and operation

According to the Forum of Federations, there are about 25 federal countries in the world. Those include some of the largest countries and most populous ones such as India, the United States, and Mexico. Thus, a large share of the world's population, 40% according to the Forum of Federations, lives in a federal country.

As Fenna outlines in his chapter, federalism is as principle of state organization: at least two orders of representative government with genuine, meaningful powers, and the existence of the orders of government and their powers are constitutionally entrenched (see also Fenna & Schnabel, 2023). The number of countries clearly fulfilling those criteria is not that large. Several countries have recently become federal — e.g., Nepal which is still in the process of implementing its federal constitution — or have had federal experiences. However, there are many countries with a quasi-federal system or at least some federal characteristics, authoritarian countries that at least claim to be federal, and countries where federalism is discussed (e.g.

Colombia). There is a wide variety of federal systems. Important dimensions on which federal countries differ is their degree of administrative or dual federalism (Mueller & Fenna, 2022) and their level of centralization and decentralization (Dardanelli et al., 2019).

How does Brazil fit in? According to Fenna, Brazil's federal nature is open to discussion. Arretche's contribution highlights particularities of the Brazilian federation. Municipalities are full members of the federation and in many areas local governments can directly negotiate with the central government circumventing the states. The Union is entitled to initiate legislation in any matter, public safety and definition of metro areas being the only exclusive powers in the hands of states. At the same time, shared responsibility prevails in several policies, which was a decisive characteristic to mitigate the impact of measures adopted by the central government during the pandemic, for example. Furthermore, as Fenna and Arretche highlight in their chapters, another challenge in many federations, including Brazil, is how to deal with territorial imbalances between wealthier and poorer constituent units, which were further exacerbated by the COVID-19 pandemic. Addressing these territorial disparities requires transfer systems, typically very complex ones. Brazil is no exception to that rule.

Another relevant topic concerning the design of Federation is second chamber. In his chapter, Souris highlights key dimensions of second chamber: selection mechanisms, territorial representation, and their powers. Although not a defining feature of federalism (see Fenna's chapter in this volume), second chambers are a prominent political institution of federal systems, despite remarkable exceptions such as Canada, where there is no chamber to represent distinct regionalist views in central government decision-making. An important question Souris raises is whether federal democracies need this kind of institution in an era of emergencies and democratic backsliding. Small territories are usually overrepresented in the second chamber, but such overrepresentation can strengthen the checks and balances and help protect minority rights, which are important characteristics of liberal democracy. The Brazilian *Senado Federal*, with its largely symmetric powers vis-à-vis the House of Representatives, is presented in Couto's chapter as a revisionary and partisan chamber rather than a federal one. Unlike other federations (e.g. Germany), smaller states are overrepresented not only in the second chamber, but also in the House of Representatives. However, when democracy is at stake, as under the Bolsonaro government, the moderation role usually expected from second chambers has the potential to hinder authoritarian initiatives.

An equally relevant issue concerning the design and operation of federations is the role of intergovernmental councils, and other types of forums formed by government representatives, which can be vertical or horizontal bodies. In her chapter, Schnabel discusses how those councils can contribute to "federal success" and draws attention to several factors that can shape their effectiveness, especially the role of the federal government, the level of institutionalization and the existence of a peak council. Grin's chapter presents four different types of intergovernmental arrangements in Brazil. First, until 2016, there was the Federative Articulation Committee, which was a vertical forum made up of generalists but without the participation of states. This was replaced, in 2023, by the Council of Federation, which convenes the three spheres of the Brazilian Federation. Second, there are five horizontal arenas formed by generalists, which are the Governors Forum and four Interstate Consortia. Third, there are also four vertical forums formed by sectoral specialists (intergovernmental councils in the areas of health, social assistance, finance and education). Finally, there are 28 other horizontal forums formed by sectoral specialists in many areas both at the state and municipal level as well as inter-municipal consortia in more than 28 policy sectors.

Regarding the Brazilian Council of Federation, Silva & Licio's chapter in this book present this intergovernmental council as a promoter of cooperation among the constituent units, as a space for negotiation, coordination, and agreement on common priority strategies and actions. This intergovernmental council has parity between the three levels of government aiming at installing a new way of thinking about the federation to deal with federal challenges such as territorial inequality. Furthermore, the Council seeks to strengthen the cooperation between the three spheres of government, considering that municipalities also are recognized as constituent units. Although its decisions are not binding, they should serve as a subsidy for the actions of the various levels of government in order to reinforce the Brazilian federation.

2. Recentralization in federations: is this a new trend?

From the 1980s onward, decentralization gained strength in several Latin American countries as well as elsewhere as a model for democratic governance and economic reforms (Wilson et al., 2009; Eaton & Dickovick, 2004). The transfer of political authority, administrative responsibilities and fiscal resources to subnational governments aimed at reducing the concentration of power at the national level in favor of greater territorial autonomy (Dickowick & Eaton, 2013). Administratively, given the scarcity of public resources in the face of social demands, decentralization was seen as a means to improve public services (Eaton, 2014). Politically, decentralization would reinforce the role of civil society, increase local management capabilities, make governments more accountable, and better manage public resources in favor of citizens' need (Rodden, 2004).

Although decentralization became increasingly associated with democracy and citizen participation, effectiveness in the provision of social policies, and subnational autonomy, in the last 30 years, there has been a recentralizing reversion in Latin America in favor of the national sphere. This phenomenon has occurred in Argentina, Brazil and Mexico, the three democratic Latin American federations (Dickovick & Eaton, 2013), and was motivated by the assumption that perceived flaws in the former decentralization process must be corrected (Bacarreza, Salas, & Martinez-Vazquez, 2021) through a more regulatory power of the federal government.

In his chapter, Olmeda discusses how the prevailing disenchantment with the previous decentralization led Mexican federal administrations to deepen recentralization in political, fiscal, and administrative dimensions. He emphasizes that recentralization is not necessarily attached to a particular ideological view and can happen even under democratic governments. Despite the substantial ideological differences between the president López Obrador (center-left/developmentalist), and the predecessor Enrique Peña Nieto (center-right/neoliberal), both adopted many recentralizing policies. In both cases, deep distrust about subnational authorities was an alleged *leitmotif* to "reorganize" the federation and reduce the autonomy of states.

In Brazil, constitutional autonomy of constituent units has declined over the last three decades. President Bolsonaro boycotted institutionalized cooperation schemes developed by the previous federal governments during the previous decades, as reported by Vazquez in his chapter. The federal government has also reduced the level of subnational discretion and autonomy in relation to rules linked to federal public policies. In many areas, but especially in welfare policies, cooperation between the federal sphere and states and municipalities has been implemented under stricter national rules and standards for implementing political programs. Furthermore, like in several other federation, such as Australia and the US (see Schnabel & Dardanelli, 2023), financial instruments with tight conditions have been used as carrots, especially for states and municipalities. In Brazil and Mexico, the COVID-19 outbreak coincided with ongoing recentralization projects and served as a lever for these political objectives. In Mexico, President López Obrador was successful, while, in Brazil, Bolsonaro was unable to implement his recentralization project since he faced successful opposition at the subnational level and from the Judiciary.

3. Federalism, diversity, innovations and challenges for democracy

For Stepan (1999), most people who live in long standing democracies live in federal systems. Does federalism promote democracy? Chattopadhyay's answer in his chapter is clearly affirmative. According to him, the "federal idea" is often at the heart of debates about democratic and inclusive governance. Federalism is even more relevant when it comes to protecting minority ethno-linguistic rights and to accommodating diversity in divided or conflict societies.

Sonnicksen's contribution to this volume draws attention to the tensions between democracy and federalism. The former is oriented more toward self-governing "people" and the latter toward self-governing "places". The complexity of this relationship can escalate in times of emergencies. A particular challenge refers to mismatches between the distribution of power and resources, on the one hand, and the actual territorial reach of problems to be addressed, on the other. Federalism also matters to refrain democratic backsliding as the division of powers between different orders of government creates constitutional and political obstacles for populist and authoritarian presidents to encroach on the autonomy of constituent units. In addition, the existence of several political communities, sometimes with distinct identities, can also be relevant to mitigate this type of political behavior.

Abrucio's chapter posits that federalism and democracy are the two main institutional parameters of contemporary Brazilian political life. Throughout Brazilian history, there have been moments of absence of both, of decoupling between the two, of fragile connection and, since 1988, there has been a growing strengthening of the coupling between federalism and democracy. This marriage has never been as strong as it is today, according to the author. However, there are still institutional cracks and weaknesses, such as the challenges regarding territorial governance on the Amazon region, due to its particularities.

Another relevant dimension is the connection between federalism and diversity. In the past, federalism was typically adopted to counter external threats and foster economic integration in large countries. This is also the case in Brazil, where a federal system was established for socioeconomic reasons and in consideration of the large size of the country. More recently, countries introducing federalism such as Belgium, Ethiopia, Nepal, or Nigeria do so because constitutionally entrenched autonomy recognizes and accommodates territorially based diversity, whether it is cultural, linguistic, or ethnic. By creating a federal system, groups with a distinct regional identity can enjoy genuine self-government. Moreover, federalism can prevent or mitigate ethnic conflict. As Chattopadhyay highlights in his chapter, federalism can help address the needs of divided societies, "providing an alternative to secession or state collapse".

This explains the relevance of federalism in several African countries. Due to their colonial heritage, the continent has many ethnic communities split in more than one country, and single countries encompassing several ethnic communities. In the 1990s, decentralization came along with pushes for democracy and efforts to accommodate ethnic groups. As Ayele describes in his chapter in this book, different federal arrangements experimented in Kenya, Ethiopia, and Nigeria have not been able to counter ethnic dominance and tensions. Nevertheless, reforms of federal institutions are still a possible way to move forward. Perhaps, one relevant lesson for Ethiopia, the most recent African federation, is the necessity to learn from Kenya and Nigeria: federal arrangements just based on ethnic lines are not the best way to organize the federal system.

In this regard, the case of Brazil may point to the opposite direction. Schlegel's contribution to this volume posits that unity still prevails in terms of territorial identity in the country, but political cleavages reflected in electoral outcomes have grown along territorial lines. Considering that defending or rejecting democracy has been a crucial divide to shape polarization in Brazil, there are risks that threats to democracy can resonate with federal issues. After all, federations are political pacts continuously built and rebuilt.

The Brazilian experience also illustrates the potential of federalism to foster democratic innovation. Subnational autonomy was important to allow states and municipalities to democratize the policy process with the diffusion of social participation initiatives, as discussed in Segatto's chapter. The central government also played a role, with incentives for the institutionalization of participatory bodies across the country. However, the recent far-right-wing administration extinguished a number of participatory bodies with a single presidential decree. Segatto's account suggests that democratic innovations are likely to be a priority target of authoritarian leaders.

4. Management of emergencies and public health policies

Federalism provides the context in which crisis management occurs in many countries. Emergencies, and especially the COVID-19 pandemic, highlight the role of subnational governments as public service providers and frontline crisis managers. Against this backdrop, emergency management has become a priority area of action for the Forum of Federations. In his chapter, Chattopadhyay posits that strong intergovernmental relations are key for effective crisis management. Ecological disasters, health crises, and other contemporary emergencies usually demand local responses, as well as coordination at higher levels of governments (Ketll, 2020). This rises the concern about the current and the ideal balance between subnational autonomy and central national response.

As Fenna highlights in his chapter in this book, the existence of two orders of government notably allows for compensation of failure of action at one level by the other. While this can be an important aspect in "normal times", it is particularly important during emergencies. As Arretche reveals in her chapter, such "compensatory federalism" was indeed at work in Brazil during the COVID-19 pandemic. While negationists at the federal level and in many states and municipalities refused to impose containment measures, leaders in other states and municipalities were able to step up; with help from the Supreme Court in what Arretche calls an "unorthodox interpretation" of the federal constitution (Arretche, 2020). Such compensation can also be important when it comes to fighting another, and perhaps the most significant, emergency that likewise confronts federal countries with distinct challenges but also highlights their advantages: climate change (Fenna, Jodoin, & Setzer, 2023).

Crises typically put the spotlight on the federal government since it commands superior financial resources. A question arises about the longer-term effect of this shift of importance vis-à-vis the constituent units.

Fiscal stimulus by the federal government usually fades and does not have long-lasting effects. As Béland argues in his chapter, however, the longer the crisis, the stronger the impact on federal relations concerning social policy—at least in Canada and the United States. Among the three major economic crises he examines, only the Great Depression led to permanent expansion of federal social policy, establishing the federal government's role in an area previously dominated by constituent units. Other crises had a less significant impact and merely consolidated the federal government's role. While those crises were shorter, the federal government's role had already been established. In younger federations, crises can have much less of a centralizing effect on social policy as the federal government usually holds some powers in that area.

Although this volume is subject to the scrutiny of time, thus aligning with changes in federations themselves, both organizers and authors aspire to provide ongoing debates with insightful contributions on Federalism and Democracy in Brazil and Beyond.

References

Abrucio, F. L. et al. (2020). Combating COVID-19 under Bolsonaro's federalism: a case of intergovernmental incoordination. *Revista de Administração Publica*, 54(4), 663-677.

Arretche, M. T. S. (2012). *Democracia, Federalismo e Centralização no Brasil*. Rio de Janeiro, RJ: Editora Fiocruz/Editora FGV.

Bacarreza, G. C., Salas, P. E., & Martinez-Vazquez, J. (2021). *The Effect of Crises on Fiscal and Political Recentralization: Large-Panel Evidence*. International Center for Public Policy. (Working Paper, pp. 21-11).

Dardanelli, P. et al. (2019). Conceptualizing, Measuring, and Theorizing Dynamic De/Centralization in Federations'. *Publius: The Journal of Federalism*, 49(1), 1-29.

Dickovick, J. T., & K. Eaton (2013). Latin America's Resurgent Centre: National Government Strategies after Decentralization. *The Journal of Development Studies*, 49(11), 1453-1466.

Eaton, K., & Dickovick, J. T. (2004). The Politics of Re-Centralization in Argentina and Brazil. *Latin American Research Review*, 39(1), 90-122.

Fenna, A., & Schnabel, J. (2023). What is Federalism? Some Definitional Clarification. *Publius: The Journal of Federalism*.

Fenna, A., Jodoin, S., & Setzer, J. (Eds.). (2023). *Climate Governance and Federalism. A Forum of Federations Comparative Policy Analysis*. Cambridge, MA: Cambridge University Press.

Fenna, A. (2022). Comparative Federalism: what is a federation and how do we study more than one?. In J. Kincaid, & J. W. Leckrone, *Teaching Federalism: multidimensional approaches* (pp. 25-33). Northampton, MA: Edward Elgar.

Hegele, Y., & Schnabel, J. (2021). Federalism and the Management of the COVID-19 Crisis: Centralisation, Decentralisation, and (Non-)Coordination. *West European Politics, 44*(5-6), 1052-1076.

Kettl, D. F. (2020). States divided: the implications of American federalism for COVID-19. *Public Administration Review, 80*(4), 595-602.

Loughlin, J., Kincaid, J., & Sweden, W. (2013). *Handbook of regionalism and federalism*. London: Routledge Taylor and Francis Group.

Mueller, S., & Fenna, A. (2022). Dual versus Administrative Federalism: Origins and Evolution of Two Models. *Publius: The Journal of Federalism, 52*(4), 525-552.

Obinger, H., Leibfried, S., & Castles, F. G. (2005). *Federalism and the welfare state: New world and European experiences*. Cambridge, MA: Cambridge University Press.

Paquet, M., & Schertzer, R. (2020). COVID-19 as a complex intergovernmental problem. *Canadian Journal of Political Science, 53*(4), 343-347.

Peters, B. G., Grin, E. J., & Abrucio, F. L. (2021). *American Federal Systems and COVID-19. Responses to a Complex Intergovernmental Problem*. Bingley: Emerald Publishing.

Rodden, J. (2004). Comparative Federalism and Decentralization: On Meaning and Measurement. *Comparative Politcs, 36*(4), 481-500.

Schnabel, J., & Dardanelli, P. (2023). Helping hand or centralizing tool? The politics of conditional grants in Australia, Canada, and the United States. *Governance: An International Journal of Policy, Administration and Institutions, 36*(3), 689-1005.

Schanabel, J. (2020). *Managing Interdependencies in Federal Systems: Intergovernmental Councils and the Making of Public Policy*. London: Pallgrave Mcmillan.

Stepan, A. (1999). Para uma Nova Análise Comparativa do Federalismo e da Democracia: Federações que Restringem ou Ampliam o Poder do Demos. *Dados – Revista de Ciências Sociais, 42*(2), 197-251.

Vazquez, D. A., & Schlegel, R. (2022). Covid-19, Fundeb e o populismo do governo Bolsonaro nas relações federativas. *Revista Brasileira de Ciência Política*, (38), e255785.

Wilson, R. H. et al. (2009). *Governance in the Americas: Decentralization, Democracy, and Subnational Government in Brazil, Mexico, and the USA*. Indiana: University of Notre Dame Press.

NEW DIRECTIONS IN THE PRACTICE OF FEDERALISM – THE ROLE OF THE FORUM OF FEDERATIONS

Rupak Chattopadhyay

Introduction

The Government of Canada provided the impetus for the establishment off the ground with the inaugural International Conference on Federalism held in 1999 at Mont Tremblant, Quebec, Canada. This conference led to the founding of The Forum as an ongoing institution, based in Ottawa. Four consecutive International Conferences have subsequently been held in Switzerland, Belgium, India, and Ethiopia. Following the 2005 Conference in Belgium and the partnership of a number of countries with The Forum, it became a truly international organization. Ten governments have now signed agreements with the Forum and are represented on the Forum's Strategic Council, supporting the activities of the organization and providing expertise. These countries are Australia, Brazil, Canada, Ethiopia, Germany, India, Mexico, Nigeria, Pakistan, and Switzerland.

Governance is the critical mechanism through which a society organizes itself, establishes the norms, value and rules of the game of public affairs, allocates resources, and engages in decision and policy making. Weak or inadequate governance inhibits development, undermines the rule of law, and leaves a society more vulnerable to bad faith actors, corruption and conflict. The Forum of Federations, as an international organization that develops and shares comparative expertise on the practice of federal and decentralized governance through a global network of federalism and governance experts, works at the forefront of federal and multilevel systems, processes and practices to support agents of change to strengthen their governance models.

Bridging theory and practice, the Forum provides those developing, refining, or simply participating in multilevel systems with the knowledge, capacity, tools and fora necessary to make informed decisions about their own approach to governance. Forum programming – wide ranging and tailored to national specificities - supports democratic and inclusive governance, based on informed decision-making, multiple power centres, cooperation among agents of change, pluralism, human rights, rule of law, gender equality and citizen involvement. In enhancing the quality and coherence of public discourse and policy as it relates to federal and multilevel governance, the Forum also supports the development of improved public service delivery and local, regional and national development strategies.

Over the last 25 years, the Forum has emerged as a platform where federations and federal type countries can come together to share experiences on how to manage, and increasingly how to set up federal systems. It is in that context that the forum first became engaged in Brazil. Over the years, we have worked with various institutions in Brazil, both at the federal level as well as with state governments, including academic institutions, and other similar groupings. Some of the work for which the Forum had laid the foundations, such as tax reform and setting up a federation council (*Conselho da Federação*), are finally coming to fruition.

Federalism and Global Emergencies

The last years, we lived through an emergency, which was the COVID pandemic. But we also have a structural emergency in terms of climate change. Taken together, these crises have had some bearing on how we think about federalism at the Forum of Federations and the work we plan for the future. About 12 years ago, the forum did some work with the Australian Emergency Management Institute, which is a think tank attached to the Federal Department of the Attorney General. We brought together disaster management specialists from nine countries. The group spent much time discussing and sharing experiences on how to deal with fires, flood, earthquakes, and even security threats. In hindsight, it is surprising that none of the countries represented even brought up the issue of pandemics. It should probably not be a surprise given that earlier pandemics like SARS had burnt themselves out without spreading beyond their regions of origin. But the COVID pandemic, is a very important inflection point for federal countries because it underscored the need for greater cooperation between levels of government and highlight the importance of delegated or devolved decision making.

Before the pandemic, I did a study for the World Bank on how different countries manage apex-level intergovernmental relations. What was remarkable in this comparative study was that in most countries there exists no statutory basis for intergovernmental relations institutions and interactions are rather ad hoc. While the Australians through their National Cabinet system are quite disciplined in coming together, in other countries, these bodies met very infrequently before the Pandemic. Indeed, the Council of Presidents in Spain or the Interstate Council in India met more frequently during the first two months of the pandemic than they had in the preceding decade and more. Arguably, therefore the pandemic provided a bit of a renaissance to governmental relations; it just became one of these emergencies where it was just impossible for any one level of government to manage this on its own.

The pandemic was also an inflection point because it showed the importance of targeted policymaking, which made it very important for subnational governments to be an important player in the process of governing. Whether or not it made the case for more federal government, it certainly made the case for more local government, particularly as service providers. This was because, as you know, the impact or the intensity of the pandemic was not uniform throughout any one country. Different parts of the country were affected differently such that big lockdowns became blunt and unsustainable policy instruments. Not surprisingly, therefore, the Forum is now working with several non-federal countries on local and metropolitan governance issues.

Federalism for the future

Twenty years ago the practitioner community, but also the academic community, had a very binary view of federalism. They saw the world as either federal or non-federal. But really systems of governance exist on a continuum. They saw federalism as the study of interaction carried out between two levels or spheres of government - a federal or national government and state or provincial government constituent units. But, of course, in practice, we know it's much more complex than that. In Brazil, for example, local governments are recognized as a constitutional order of government. This is true in some other countries such as India, Nigeria and Mexico, but none of them are as autonomous as in Brazil. And, even given what I've just said about the role of local governments in the pandemic, more and more in countries where local governments are not constitutionalized, they're a very important player in the intergovernmental space. In addition to that, in some countries indigenous government is a very important player in the scheme of intergovernmental relations. So, for us, this is a very important area of investigation into the future.

Think what you may of Elon Musk, but one of the most insightful things he ever said at the World Economic Forum meeting some years ago was that population implosion is the greatest threat to the future prosperity of mankind. And we realize now, certainly in many parts of the world, that we may have to live with some level of structural inflation because we cannot find enough trained people for jobs that are needed. So, this has opened up for us the need to think about how one can fill in all these missing people going forward. The COVID pandemic brought to the forefront the issue of worker shortages, particularly at the retail end of business (commercial and government).

This, in turn, has caused more governments to focus on the issue of digitization of service delivery and on Artificial Intelligence as a force multiplier. The Forum is already doing a project on digital government, and I think over time this will gain greater salience in terms of the role that digitization can play in easing government services. But there are a lot of issues that must be sorted out in terms of ownership of data, access and privacy. All these issues, in many parts of the world, multiple levels of government are already fighting over. I had the privilege some months ago of attending a foresight conference organized by the government of United Arab Emirates. Many European countries are beginning to think again within the context of population explosion, how they're going to replace frontline workers in frontline services with respect to the provision of social services and more and more many seem to think about that. However, there is no clarity yet really, on how this might happen, but the fact that people are thinking about it. It is important because this too will have some of the concerns that digital government has raised around regulation, about data ownership, privacy and really the space for some national governments to play.

While the most of these antecedent conditions around governance challenges and state fragility predate COVID-19, the pandemic and its associated impacts both accelerated these trends and brought into sharper focus the threats they represent to individual countries and the international community. The cascading economic and social impacts of the COVID pandemic have been significant and exacerbated existing tensions and crises with damaging effects. The prospect of a global economic slowdown, recession, combined with an inflation and cost of living crisis in many of the world's most advanced economies, is likely to squeeze access to public goods in many countries. Social discontent is increasing in many parts of the world, manifest by a rise in often violent protest. Disillusionment with status quo politics has undermined trust in governance institutions and widened the gap for anti-democratic actors to exploit vulnerabilities and erode democratic systems. This in turn poses a threat to the fostering of more inclusive societies in which women and girls, as well as ethnic, linguistic and religious minorities, are full and equal participants in society and politics. The devastating impact of climate change presents an existential threat that compounds the existing challenges such as water scarcity, and creates new ones concerning food security and natural disasters.

While many of these threats are transnational in nature, addressing the impacts and ensuring that people continue to receive the services they need requires governments, decision makers, and agents of change equipped with the knowledge and capacity necessary to develop and implement effective policy. Indeed, it is unlikely there will be a single solution to any of these multi-faceted and interconnected threats. This is particularly pertinent in federal and multilevel systems, in which different governments have the autonomy to develop and implement policies tailored to the specifics conditions and needs of a municipality, province, state or region.

Federalism and Democracy

The last issue that I want to touch on is democracy. Does federalism promote democracy or not? Let me start by saying the first thing is certainly yes. The Forum acts as a platform for learning amongst federal countries, but we also do a lot of work in post-conflict settings and in what I would call emerging federal democracies. In rare cases it's possible to have federal system that is not democratic or at least have a system that or there are systems where there is what I would call a democratic deficit. But in most of these post-conflict situations, it's first about ending the conflict and coming to an agreement on the division of powers. But if you then don't follow that up with some kind of democratic setup, these are temporary solutions are doomed to fail. So, the sequencing question is a big question. Over the last 25 odd years, I am increasingly coming to the conclusion, depressing as it may be, that I don't think the world is about to converge on liberal democracy. Liberal democracy is the product of very specific historical processes, but it looks like we will converge more and more towards representative government in some way or the other. Federalism plays a very important role in countries in preventing democratic backsliding acting. Even in more non-federal countries the movement towards further devolution and decentralization exists not just because for normative reasons, but because this provides an opportunity for governments to be more responsible on service delivery.

The Forum's experience over the last 20 years has demonstrated the continued relevance of federalism, federal type and multilevel systems of governance. Indeed, a steady expansion of countries where the Forum's expertise has been in demand beyond the classic federations, shows that the "federal idea" is often at the heart of debates about democratic and inclusive governance. This is particularly true where debates coalesce around issues of unity and diversity as well as arising from questions of ethno-linguistic accommodation. Federalism provides a toolkit of solutions, which in whole or part may be applied to address internal conflict and to address challenges in divided societies, providing an alternative to secession or state collapse.

Since 1945, a remarkable number of countries have become federal, and several others have moved in that direction. However, there have also been numerous failed attempts at federalism. It is the ambition of the Forum to share and learn from these experiences to support the development of federal and multilevel systems fit to meet global challenges.

FEDERALISM AND FEDERATIONS: AN INTRODUCTORY OVERVIEW

Alan Fenna

This chapter provides a schematic overview of federalism and federations, their structure and functioning, and lays some foundations for the contributions that follow. It begins with the very basic but important question 'what is federalism?' — a question that has proven surprisingly vexed. It then turns to questions of constitutional design, notably the division of powers and bicameralism; questions of political practice, such as intergovernmental relations and fiscal federalism; and finally questions of political effects, such as the relationship between federalism and democracy and the operation of federal systems in emergency situations.

What is Federalism?

Federalism is an organizational principle or form with three defining characteristics (Fenna & Schnabel, 2024). The first is that a federation is a state, with a clear international identity and sovereign powers; it is not a looser arrangement. Secondly, it is a state whose territory is divided into self-governing jurisdictions or 'constituent units' — provinces, states, *Länder*, cantons, Autonomous Communities or whatever else they may be called. And the third defining feature is that those constituent units enjoy a genuine degree of meaningful autonomy. Daniel Elazar (1987, p. 5) summed this up in his notion that federalism is 'the combination of self-rule and shared rule'. The constituent units enjoy a degree of 'self-rule' while the central government provides an overarching 'shared rule'.

Federal vs confederal

The first criterion distinguishes federations from looser associations, such a confederations or leagues, where the locus of sovereignty remains the constituent units rather than the union. Confederal arrangements have a long history, with the Swiss Confederacy, which lasted from 1291 to 1798, being the prime example. They are much rarer today, with the European Union being the closest example, albeit one 'evolving' toward federalism (Eppler, 2020). The United Arab Emirates is also more confederal than it is federal (Simmons, 2020). Argentina, Brazil and Mexico meet this first criterion (Farah, Piepel, & Griffiths, 2020; Souza, 2020; Rojas, 2020).

Federal vs unitary

The second criterion is that the state is divided into self-governing regions. In the original 'coming together' federations, of which only a few pure cases exist (e.g., Australia, United States), these pre-existed and created the union from below. In 'holding together' federations, these were established from above. Argentina, Brazil and Mexico can be described as holding-together federations (Stepan, 1999).

A complicating aspect here is that federal states typically have three orders of government: central, regional and local. In the majority of federations, local government has little or no constitutional status and comes under the authority of the constituent units (Steytler, 2024b). This is the case, for instance, in Australia, Canada and the United States. Given, in particular, that some cities are enormous, this exclusion can seem anomalous (Hirschl, 2020). Brazil and South Africa stand out as federations that give local government constitutional status, but in doing so they illustrate the extent to which such recognition undermines federalism by hollowing out the constituent units and thereby privileging the central government (Steytler, 2024a).

While division of the country into self-governing regions is a hallmark of federalism, many unitary states have regional governments of some form. Thus, of decisive importance is the third criterion: the constituent units must have genuine autonomy. That autonomy comes in the form of constitutionally protected status and meaningful powers and access to resources. In the UK, a famously unitary state, significant powers of self-government have been delegated to Scotland and Wales, but the locus of sovereignty remains Westminster (Keating, 2016). Likewise in Italy, significant powers have been delegated to regional governments, but only the special regions have a status that amounts to federalism (Delladonne, Monti, & Martinico, 2021; Palermo, 2012). An interesting example is Spain, a country that is regarded by some scholars as indeed a federation (e.g., Sala, 2014), although it does not describe itself as one. However, it remains an open question whether the Autonomous Communities have meaningful autonomy (Colino, 2020; Anderson, 2022).

Then there are countries that are ostensibly federal, but where the autonomy of the constituent units is so reduced or compromised as to render them substantively unitary. Russia is a prime example (Ross, 2022). In such cases, there is a symbolic structure of federalism, and these may be useful politically within the country, but in reality there is little or no federal practice because of autocratic government and central control, the oppressive character of a one-party state. Another such case is Ethiopia (Fessha, 2019). Whether there is sufficient autonomy of the constituent units in Argentina, Brazil and Mexico for these countries to be truly federal is a matter for discussion.

The Division of Powers

Given that constituent unit autonomy is at the heart of what makes a federal system, nothing is more pivotal to federal design and operation than the division of powers. This may be structured in either of two ways and it tends to follow a certain logic whereby responsibility for matters that are local in scale are assigned to the constituent units.

Dual versus Administrative Federalism

When we look around the world, we see two kinds of ideal-typical models (Mueller & Fenna, 2022; Hueglin & Fenna, 2015). One is the 'dualist' model, developed in the United States and practiced particularly in Australia and Canada, where the two orders of government are assigned full policy making, implementation, and administration powers within defined policy domains; they exercise both legislative and administrative responsibility. The archetypal other model, the German, is of administrative division of powers whereby in many domains, the division is not between policy *fields*, but between *functions* or *roles*. In many of the areas where the central government is assigned jurisdiction, it exercises an overarching legislative responsibility for policy making but must rely on the constituent units for implementation and administration.

Blurring of the lines

In principle, they are two quite different models, but over time, there has been an erosion of the distinction, particularly because of the evolution of the dualist federations (Mueller & Fenna, 2022). More and more tasks of government have become broader in scale and seen as having a national dimension so central governments have tended to intervene to shape policy in areas of constituent unit responsibility while leaving delivery of services in constituent unit hands. This has driven a historical process of centralisation across the older federations (Dardanelli et al., 2019; see also Moscovich & Eussler, 2023; Olmeda, 2023; Schlegel, 2023).

Subsidiarity

Guiding the division of powers is an implicit principle of 'subsidiarity', the principle that whatever can be done effectively and efficiently at the lower level should be done at the lower level. Subsidiarity is the normative principle that underpins the federal idea. While reality is too complex for the principle to be applied easily, it nonetheless informs federal thinking on the question.

Adjudication

A system where powers are divided between two orders of government inevitably gives rise to differences and disputes and this necessarily implies some mechanism of adjudication. In almost all cases, federal systems include, then, a legal umpire in the form of an independent judiciary empowered to disallow ordinary legislation on constitutional grounds[2]. Indeed, the very principle of judicial review emerged from the very early US experience with federalism. Judicial review has come to play a significant role in the evolution of federal systems (Aroney & Kincaid, 2017). To play its role fairly, that umpire should be neutral and not structurally biased toward one side or the other. Thus, the process for appointment to courts that have the final say on constitutional interpretation is an important element in the design of federal systems.

---

[2] Almost' because Switzerland is a partial exception to this, perhaps the world's most iconic federation, but one where the federal government is not subordinate to rulings on these sorts of federal issues, not subordinate to a Supreme Court or a constitutional court.

Bicameralism

Another prominent design feature of federal systems is bicameralism, or, more specifically, second-chamber representation of the constituent units. However, it is not one that has proven as important as is often assumed to the operation of federal systems. There is a strong affinity between federalism and bicameralism. In part this reflects the central place accorded to the Senate in settling on a compromise for the pioneering US Constitution. In part it reflects the prevalence of second chambers in the world's federal systems. And in part it reflects an implicit logic that the constituent units should have an avenue through which they can represent and protect their interests within the deliberations of the central government. In practice, while almost universal, those second chambers vary enormously in what role they play, what powers they have, and to the extent to which they can be described as territorially representative. Indeed, the only second chamber in the world that has a genuinely federal character is the German *Bundesrat*, where the executive governments of the constituent units, the *Länder*, are represented. By providing the *Länder* with a veto power over legislative that concerns them, the *Bundesrat* complements Germany's system of administrative federalism. This question of federal bicameralism is pursued in greater length in the chapter by Antonios Souris in this volume.

More common in federal second chambers than direct representation of the constituent units is equal representation regardless of population. This was the model settled upon by the Americans and mimicked in other federations such as Australia, Switzerland, Argentina and Brazil. It has the effect of giving low-population jurisdictions disproportionate representation, sometimes massively so, but otherwise it is not clear what federal quality it imparts.

Intergovernmental Relations

With the exception of Germany and its federal second chamber, the early federations made little provision for interaction between the orders of government. It was assumed that the each would operate within its respective sphere and little interaction would need to occur. The reality of federal practice has become very different from this, with the complexity and extent of government tasks as well as shifting jurisdictional reach making interaction unavoidable. A 'cooperative federalism' of negotiation, conflict, coordination, and collaboration by necessity prevails.

Intergovernmental relations have become a firmly established but almost entirely extra-constitutional practice of federal systems. Particularly in parliamentary federations, it typically comprises peak level meetings between heads of government and the establishment of portfolio ministerial councils (Poirier, Saunders, & Kincaid, 2015; Schnabel, 2020). A manifestation may be formal intergovernmental agreements, which while not having the force of law are nonetheless significant political and administrative documents. These practices are explained further in Chapter 12 by Johanna Schnabel in this volume.

Fiscal Federalism

It is one thing to have a specified division of powers on paper and in the Constitution, but when push comes to shove, it's typically money that counts. Fiscal federalism is thus crucial to understanding the operation of any federal system. The issue presents itself on two planes. Vertically, there is the question of the respective resourcing and financial relationship between the two orders of government. Horizontally, there is the question of the sharing of wealth among the constituent units. Both have been troublesome.

The vertical dimension

Most prescriptive federalism theory holds that access to revenue should be aligned with the allocation of responsibilities. If the constituent units have a certain task to do, then they should have access to the tax revenue to execute that task. However, that is not what often happens — primarily because it is much easier to levy most taxes effectively across a whole country than it is at the constituent-unit level. The result is *vertical fiscal imbalance* (VFI), where the central government has access to tax revenues that it controls in considerable excess of its spending needs, and vice versa for the constituent units to have spending responsibilities that they cannot fund out of their own revenue[3]. At the extreme stands Australia, where the central government collects over 80 per cent of all tax revenue. The situation is less extreme in Brazil, but, at 70 per cent, still pronounced (Rezende, Cialdini, & Motta, 2023, p. 76). The result is a reliance in such federations on transfers to the constituent units from central governments.

---

[3] An exception is the EU, where, as a more confederal system, the 'central government' depends on transfers from the member states.

These transfers can take, generally speaking, one of two forms. The first is unconditional or general-purpose funding — which is what the autonomy rule would prescribe. However, the temptation for central governments to use those grants as an instrument for influencing policy within areas of constituent unit jurisdiction is often too great to resist and, depending on the federation, and thus the second form is conditional or specific-purpose funding. In Australia, for instance, conditional grants make up 50% of all the transfers to the States and the central (Commonwealth) government uses them to influence policy in various areas of state government jurisdiction. Conditional grants have long been a major prominent element of American federalism as well. In other federations, there are other means of addressing this problem, regarding the vertical dimension of the fiscal problem.

The horizontal dimension

In addition to vertical fiscal inequalities, federal systems are also bedevilled by horizontal ones. In some federations more so than others, there is a substantial economic and fiscal disparity from one constituent unit to next. This is the case in Brazil, for instance. Almost all federations, then, practise formally some form of *horizontal fiscal equalisation*, whereby money is redistributed across the country on the principle that there is an entitlement of citizenship to a certain standard of public services wherever one resides. The notable exception is the United States.

There is also a practical logic behind this: if a number of constituent units are very poor and do not have access to the resources necessary to provide the kind of services citizens want, then there is a strong pressure on the central government to move in and provide those services itself, which tends to undermine the principle of federalism. Not having equalisation invites more federal intervention. Without such intervention, there is unlikely to be the level of citizen-based social provision across the country that is expected or desired. Thus, there is a practical argument as well as a moral or citizenship argument in favour of equalisation.

The problem with equalisation is that the politics is rather different from the moral aspect. This is a highly visible zero-sum game with money flowing from one jurisdiction to another. This transparency problem is potentially exacerbated by two things. One is the degree of disparity. If the disparities are modest then so is the challenge. But if the disparities are large, that accentuates the political problem. Moreover, if a small *per capita* amount is being transferred to a jurisdiction with a large population, that ends up to being a very large amount. Canada is a case in point (Fenna, 2023a). In Australia, for most of the history of the equalisation system, rich jurisdictions were also the two demographically dominant jurisdictions, so they had to give up only a very small proportion of their aggregate to help out the smaller, poorer jurisdictions. Then the tables turned a bit and one of the low population jurisdictions became rich, which meant it had to give up a huge amount of its wealth to help compensate the rest of the country. Such accidents of history have a major impact on how equalisation works.

Then there is the question of how thoroughly the system seeks to equalise. Australia and Germany have long practised a thorough-going equalisation, while Canada and Switzerland have taken a compromise approach. In both Australia and Germany, the system was put under pressure when demands increased.

Finally, there are the means by which it is carried out. The most explicit mode of equalisation is to transfer directly from rich jurisdictions to poorer ones. That is really making it patently and transparently zero sum. The Canadian system, by contrast, is indirect, such that the funding for equalization comes out of the federal government budget rather than being explicitly transferred from province to province. However, what the rich province may well then say is yes, but we pay disproportionately into your budget, so we're still being robbed; but at least it's a little bit less transparent. In the Australian system there is a pool of tax revenue raised by the central government assigned to the states that is divided up between them to adjust for disparities between their fiscal capacities and their spending needs.

Borrowing

The remaining aspect of fiscal federalism we have to keep in mind is not just taxing and spending, but also public borrowing, and this has been at various times a problem in federal systems. Unconstrained borrowing by constituent units may destabilise the country fiscally. Various mechanisms and approaches have evolved over the years to reduce this risk. One is the sink or swim approach. If a constituent unit borrows imprudently and goes bankrupt, that is its problem. This has been the US or Canadian approach.

The other approach is paternalistic regulation from above, some sort of joint borrowing arrangement, involving regulation and control over borrowing at the constituent unit level is. That has been until recently the Australian practice.

Federalism and Democracy

A broader question to which this book returns in Sonnicksen's chapter in this volume is the relationship between federalism and democracy. The country that pioneered modern federalism was also the first modern democracy, but at the same time went on to provide stark example of how federalism might be anti-democratic. Does federalism require democracy, and, vice versa, does democracy benefit from federalism?

The importance of democracy to federalism

There are many reasons to think that a properly functioning or truly federal system requires a properly functioning liberal democracy with the rule of law and a reasonably competitive party system. This is primarily because federalism assumes constitutionalism and a rules-based order — that these will be respected and not overridden by political forces. There is thus a very strong argument that federalism does require democracy. A number of the faux federations mentioned above, such as Russia, are so precisely because of their democratic deficits.

The implications of federalism for democracy

And then, vice-versa, is democracy enhanced by federalism? This is in some ways a more interesting question, one to which there is no simple answer. It depends on other broader aspects of the political system. On the one hand, federalism enhances democracy by including a second tier of governments, thereby bringing government closer to the people, generating a closer democratic connection. In addition, the two orders of government can provide some sort of checks and balances against each other. These are both plausible propositions, and there are some supporting examples, but it need not be the case. And particularly, it may not be the case since federalism is about maintaining the autonomy of the constituent units.

What if that autonomy then allows those constituent units to continue with practices that are contrary to democracy? At various times federalism has exhibited the potential to harbour illiberal and undemocratic practices (Behrend & Whitehead, 2016; Gibson, 2013). There is no better case in that respect than the United States, where one federalism scholar said in the 1960s if you are a federalist, you are a racist, because federalism allows the segregationist racism of the American South (Riker, 1964, p. 155). In a more quotidian way, federalism has been accused of working against democracy by reducing the accountability of individual governments because of the extent to which responsibilities are entangled and obscured (e.g., Benz, 2015).

Final thoughts: federalism and emergencies

What about federalism and public policy, specifically 'emergencies'? As with the implications of federalism for democracy, that answer is that 'it depends'. There are at least three ways in which federalism can enhance the response to public policy challenges: its fail-safe potential; its invitation to localised responses; and the scope it provides for policy learning.

Redundancy

First is the potential benefit of having two tiers of government (or more). In what has been labelled 'compensatory federalism', existence of two orders of government with overlapping powers offers a potentially valuable fail-safe potential (Derthick, 2010). Should the central government fail to act, the constituent units can provide a back-up — compensating for inaction at the central government level. Illustration can be found in both climate change policy and the management of COVID 19. In both cases we see examples in different countries where there was inaction at the central government level. In Australia, for example, the states stepped up and took a very active role — and in fact carried forward collectively a *de facto* national policy on climate change — when the federal government was opposed to taking action (Fenna, 2023b). A similar dynamic was evident in Brazil during the pandemic (Néris & Bedritichuk, 2021).

Local variation

Then there's the second potential benefit of federalism: having scope for a devolved response, a regionally-calibrated response. We often think of fragmentation as undesirable or detrimental, but it offers possible benefits. Some of these benefits can be seen in climate change and COVID. In climate change, because their economic structure may well differ significantly from region to region, the ability of individual constituent units to tailor policies has a particular attraction. With COVID, it was often the case that the impact varied from jurisdiction to jurisdiction, so the appropriate strategy varied accordingly.

In addition, the ability to quarantine a problem to within one part of the country is greater in a federal system — something that proved its worth during the pandemic. Again, in Australia for instance, one state was very hard hit and in response the other states closed their borders to minimise transmission (Fenna, 2021). There federalism allowed a real quarantining.

Policy learning

Federalism also provides scope for interjurisdictional learning. Policy makers and the public in general can look at what is being implemented in other jurisdictions and make informed judgements about what works best. Ideally, they eschew the unsuccessful and borrow the successful. However, such judgements are not always easy to make, and assessment is rarely free of ideological preferences. The evidence is slim for how much of this type of learning actually occurs, but it cannot be denied that the potential is there.

Downsides

One would be remiss not to acknowledge, on the other side of the ledger, the potential costs and downsides to federalism and a devolved response. One of is particularly evident in climate change policy, where the efforts of conscientious jurisdictions working in the collective interest may well be outweighed the actions of others acting in their self-interest. This is precisely what has been happening in both Canada and Brazil, where some jurisdictions have been working hard on emissions reduction, while others continue contributing enormously to the problem itself (Harrison, 2023; Seleguim & Rei, 2023). In such situations, there is thus the perennial risk of shirking. And, to bring things back to intergovernmental relations, there is always the challenge of getting governments to work effectively together. Sometimes autonomous action is cumulative across jurisdictions, but often to be effective it requires cooperation and coordination, if not indeed collaboration.

References

Anderson, P. (2022). Spain and the United Kingdom: Between unitary state tradition and federalization. In S. Keil, & S. Kropp (Eds.), Emerging Federal Structures in the Post-Cold War Era (pp. 49-72). London: Springer.

Aroney, N., & Kincaid, J. (Eds.). (2017). *Courts in Federal Countries: Federalists or unitarists?* Toronto: University of Toronto Press.

Behrend, J., & Whitehead, L. (2016). Illiberal Practices: Territorial variance within large federal democracies. New York City: Johns Hopkins University Press.

Benz, A. (2015). Making democracy work in a federal system. *German Politics, 24*(1), 8-11.

Colino, C. (2020). Decentralization in Spain: Federal evolution and performance of the Estado autonómico. In D. Muro, & I. Lago (Eds.), *The Oxford Handbook of Spanish Politics* (pp. 62-81). Oxford: Oxford University Press.

Dardanelli, P. et al. (2019). Dynamic de/centralization in federations: Comparative conclusions. *Publius: The Journal of Federalism, 49*(1), 194-219.

Delladonne, G., Monti, M., & Martinico, G. (2021). Subnational constitutionalism in Italy: Unfulfilled expectations? In P. Popelier, N. Aroney, & G. Delledonne (Eds.), *The Routledge Handbook of Subnational Constitutions and Constitutionalism* (pp. 176-191). London: Routledge.

Derthick, M. (2010). Compensatory federalism. In B. G. Rabe (Ed.), *Greenhouse Governance: Addressing climate change in America* (pp. 58-72). Washington, DC: Brookings Institution Press.

Elazar, D. J. (1987). *Exploring Federalism.* University of Alabama Press.

Eppler, A. (2020). European Union: Evolving from a free trade area to federalism. In A. Griffiths, R. Chattopadhyay, J. Light, & C. Stieren (Eds.), *The Forum of Federations Handbook of Federal Countries* (pp. 147-166). London: Springer.

Farah, P., Pieper, M., & Griffiths, A. (2020). Argentina (Argentine Republic): Balancing centralization with federalism. In A. Griffiths, R. Chattopadhyay, J. Light, & C. Stieren (Eds.), *The Forum of Federations Handbook of Federal Countries*. (pp. 17-28). London: Springer.

Fenna, A. (2021). Australian federalism and the COVID-19 crisis. In R. Chattopadhyay, F. Knüpling, D. Chebenova, L. Whittington, & P. Gonzalez (Eds.), Federalism and the Response to COVID-19: A comparative analysis (pp. 17-29). London: Routledge.

Fenna, A. (2023a). Canadian fiscal federalism in comparative perspective. In A. Lecours, D. Béland, T. Tombe, & E. Champagne (Eds.), *Fiscal Federalism in Canada: Analysis, evaluation, prescription* (pp. 451-475). University of Toronto Press.

Fenna, A. (2023b). Climate governance and federalism in Australia. In A. Fenna, S. Jodoin, & J. Setzer (Eds.), *Climate Governance and Federalism: A Forum of Federations comparative policy analysis* (pp. 14-40). Cambridge, MA: Cambridge University Press.

Fenna, A., & Schnabel, J. (2024). What is federalism? Some definitional clarification. *Publius: The Journal of Federalism*, 2 (54): 179-200.

Fessha, Y. T. (2019). A federation without federal credentials: The story of federalism in a dominant-party state. In C. M. Fombad, & N. Steytler (Eds.), *Decentralisation and Constitutionalism in Africa* (pp. 133-150). Oxford: Oxford University Press.

Gibson, E. L. (2013). *Boundary control: Subnational authoritarianism in federal democracies*. Cambridge University Press.

Harrison, K. (2023). Climate governance and federalism in Canada. In A. Fenna, S. Jodoin, & J. Setzer (Eds.), *Climate Governance and Federalism: A Forum of Federations comparative policy analysis*. Cambridge, MA: Cambridge University Press.

Hirschl, R. (2020). City, State: Constitutionalism and the megacity. Oxford University Press.

Hueglin, T. O., & Fenna, A. (2015). *Comparative Federalism: A systematic inquiry* (2nd ed.). Toronto: University of Toronto Press.

Keating, M. (2016). Why is there no federalism in the United Kingdom? In A. G. Gagnon, S. Keil, & S. Mueller (Eds.), *Understanding Federalism and Federation* (pp. 177-191). London: Routledge.

Moscovich, L., & Eussler, S. L. (2023). De/centralization in Argentina, 1862–2020. *Regional & Federal Studies, 33*(5), 607-635.

Mueller, S., & Fenna, A. (2022). Dual versus administrative federalism: Origins and evolution of two models. *Publius: The Journal of Federalism, 52*(4), 525-552.

Néris, E. H. C. da S. P., & Bedritichuk, R. R. (2021). Brazilian federalism: Facing the COVID-19 pandemic. In R. Chattopadhyay, F. Knüpling, D. Chebenova, L. Whittington, & P. Gonzalez (Eds.), *Federalism and the Response to COVID-19: A comparative analysis* (pp. 59-65). London: Routledge.

Olmeda, J. C. (2023). De/centralization in Mexico, 1824–2020. *Regional & Federal Studies, 33*(5), 671-698.

Palermo, F. (2012). Italy: A federal country without federalism? In M. Burgess, & G. A. Tarr (Eds.), *Constitutional Dynamics in Federal Systems*: Sub-national perspectives (pp. 237-254). Montreal: McGill-Queen's University Press.

Poirier, J., Saunders, C., & Kincaid, J. (Eds.). (2015). *Intergovernmental Relations in Federal Systems: Comparative structures and dynamics*. Oxford: Oxford University Press.

Rezende, F., Cialdini, A., & Motta, B. (2023). Brazil. In J.-F. Tremblay (Ed.), The Forum of Federations Handbook of Fiscal Federalism (pp. 59–95).

Riker, W. H. (1964). *Federalism: Origin, Operation, Significance.* Boston: Little, Brown and Company.

Rodden, J. (2006). Hamilton's Paradox: The promise and peril of fiscal federalism. Cambridge University Press.

Rojas, D. B. (2020). Mexico (Mexican United States). In A. Griffiths, R. Chattopadhyay, J. Light, & C. Stieren (Eds.), *The Forum of Federations Handbook of Federal Countries 2020* (pp. 215–225). Cham: Springer.

Ross, C. (2022). Federalism and De-Federalisation in Russia. In G. Gill (Ed.), *Routledge Handbook of Russian Politics and Society*. Abingdon: Routledge.

Sala, G. (2014). Federalism without Adjectives in Spain. *Publius,* 44(1), 109–134.

Schlegel, R. (2023). Dynamic De/Centralization in Brazil, 1889–2020: The Prevalence of Punctuated Centralization. *Regional & Federal Studies,* 33(5), 637–669.

Seleguim, F. B., & Rei, F. (2023). Climate Governance and Federalism in Brazil. In A. Fenna, S. Jodoin, & J. Setzer (Eds.), *Climate Governance and Federalism: A Forum of Federations Comparative Policy Analysis* (pp. 41–63). Cambridge: Cambridge University Press.

Simeon, R. (2016). Federal-provincial diplomacy: The making of recent policy in Canada. Toronto: University of Toronto Press.

Simmons, J. M. (2020). United Arab Emirates: Centralization and Prosperity Before Democracy. In A. Griffiths, R. Chattopadhyay, J. Light, & C. Stieren (Eds.), *The Forum of Federations Handbook of Federal Countries* (pp. 353–366).

Souza, C. (2020). Brazil (Federative Republic of Brazil): Federalism After Centralization and New Constitutions. In A. Griffiths, R. Chattopadhyay, J. Light, & C. Stieren (Eds.), *The Forum of Federations Handbook of Federal Countries 2020* (pp. 83–95). Cham: Springer.

Skogstad, G. (2011). Canadian federalism and the governance of genetically modified foods. In H. Bakvis, & G. Skogstad (Eds.), *Canadian Federalism: Performance, effectiveness, and legitimacy* (3rd ed., pp. 225–245). Oxford: Oxford University Press.

Stepan, A. (1999). Federalism and Democracy: Beyond the U.S. Model. *Journal of Democracy*, 10(4), 19–34.

Steytler, N. (2024a). Comparative Conclusions. In N. Steytler (Ed.), *The Forum of Federations Handbook on Local Government in Federal Systems* (pp. 533–586). Cham: Palgrave Macmillan.

Steytler, N. (Ed.). (2024b). *The Forum of Federations Handbook on Local Government in Federal Systems.* Cham: Palgrave Macmillan.

Swenden, W., & McEwen, N. (Eds.). (2014). *Territorial Politics in Hard Times: Comparative territorial politics.* London: Palgrave Macmillan.

Watts, R. L. (1999). *Comparing Federal Systems* (2nd ed.). McGill-Queen's University Press.

Wheare, K. C. (1963). Federal Government (4th ed.). Oxford: Oxford University Press.

FEDERALISM AND FEDERATIONS: THE BRAZILIAN PERSPECTIVE

Marta Arretche

Introduction

This chapter presents the institutional choices of the constitutional framers in Brazil, aiming to better inform those that are not familiar with Brazilian institutions. I will also discuss what I consider to be the main divide of Brazilian federalism. Consequently, I will examine how the Brazilian federal state operates, and then I will offer some observations on what we have learned from COVID-19 and our experience in preventing democratic backsliding.

Brazil comprises a central government, 26 states, a federal district, and nearly 5,570 municipalities, making it a large federation. It is crucial to understand that both local governments and states hold the same political status, meaning that unlike most federations municipalities are not subordinate to states. Therefore, in many aspects, local governments are directly connected to the central government. Another important aspect is that despite significant differences in the size of municipalities, they all must have the same administrative format. For instance, while the city of São Paulo has nearly 12 million inhabitants, more than 20% of Brazilian municipalities shelter less than 5,000 inhabitants. However, according to the Constitution, they all have the same administrative status and must be governed under the same administrative arrangements.

Another particularity of the Brazilian Federation is that the Union is entitled to initiate legislation on any matter (except public safety and metropolitan areas, which are exclusive of states). This means that the central government can be very active in setting the rules in any area of public policy. While any level of government can indeed formulate policy in any area, in practice, to simplify a complex topic, the Union (encompassing the executive, the legislative and the judiciary branches) is constitutionally empowered to establish the regulations for most policies that subnational governments are responsible for.

All three levels of governments are involved in most public policies, but states and municipalities are primarily active in service provision policies. However, this does not mean that the central government is absent. On the contrary, the central government is very active in setting the regulations and funding the provision of policies, while municipalities are mainly responsible for their implementation. In other words, subnational governments are autonomous, except in areas where the federal level sets the rules under which policies will be implemented, and there are many such areas.

Some examples can help illustrate this setting. For instance, a discussion on tax reform related to consumption was recently held in the Brazilian parliament [the seminar was held in June 2023]. Although the taxation of goods and services is under the exclusive jurisdiction of states and municipalities, the tax reform is being deliberated in the federal Congress, at the level of the Union. Currently, most states have their own lists of basic items exempt from taxation on goods. If this reform is eventually approved [which was in December 2023], a unique list, determined at the federal level, of basic items exempt from consumption tax will be established [a prevision that was ultimately confirmed].

Another example is the healthcare system, in which states and municipalities are responsible for delivering health services. Therefore, states and municipalities are heavily involved in providing healthcare services and funding them with their own revenues. Nevertheless, they must adhere to a lengthy list of rules set by the federal Constitution, which limits their ability to innovate.

Table 1. Authority of regional gov'ts and representatives over the region (self-rule) and the whole country (shared rule)

	SELF-RULE				SHARED RULE			
	Policy scope[1]	Taxation[2]	Borrow[3]	Subnational elections[4]	Territorial symmetrical chamber[5]	Partisan senators[6]	Veto on revenue distribution[7]	Constitutional rigidity[8]
				FEDERAL				
Argentina	Yes	Yes	Yes	Yes	Yes	Yes	Yes	Yes
Brazil	Yes	No	No	Yes	Yes	Yes	Yes	No
Mexico	Yes	No	Yes	Yes	Yes	Yes	No	Yes
Venezuela	No	No	No	No	No	--	No	Yes

	SELF-RULE			SHARED RULE				
	Policy scope[1]	Taxation[2]	Borrow[3]	Subnational elections[4]	Territorial symmetrical chamber[5]	Partisan senators[6]	Veto on revenue distribution[7]	Constitutional rigidity[8]
UNITARY								
Bolivia	Yes	Yes	No	Yes	Yes	Yes	No	Yes
Chile	No	No	No	No	Yes	Yes	No	No
Colombia	Yes	No	No	Yes	No	Yes	No	No
Ecuador	Yes	No	No	Yes	No	--	No	No
Guatemala	No	No	No	No	No	--	No	No
Honduras	No	No	No	No	No	--	No	No
Nicaragua	Yes	Yes	No	Yes	No	--	No	No
Paraguay	No	No	No	Yes	No	Yes	No	Yes
Peru	Yes	No	No	Yes	No	--	No	No
Dominican Republic	No	No	No	Yes	Yes	Yes	No	No
Uruguay	Yes	No	No	Yes	No	Yes	No	Yes

Source: Hooghe et al. (2016); Llanos (2003); National Constitutions
(1) Subnational government has authoritative competences in at least two of the following competences: (a) economic policy; (b) cultural-educational policy; (c) welfare policy; (d) institutional-coercive policy
(2) Authority to set own taxes and rates
(3) Authority to borrow without previous central government consent
(4) The subnational executive is directly elected or appointed by a directly elected assembly
(5) Subnational representatives have institutional decision-making on revenue distribution
(6) Senate is a territorial house + Senate approval is required for any matter + disagreement between houses is solved by joint deliberation
(7) Senators are elected through parties
(8) Referendum/state-level assemblies' approval or constitutional assembly is required to change (even partially) the constitution
Note: Includes all democratic countries with more than 8 million inhabitants

Table 1 is based upon the taxonomy of the RAI project lead by Liesbet Hooghe, Gary Marks and Arjan Schakel. The table clearly shows that the institutions of the Brazilian federation are closer to those adopted by large Latin America unitary polities than to Latin American federations in terms of the self-rule dimension. States and municipalities in Brazil are not allowed to create new taxes other than those authorized by the federal

Constitution. They also are not allowed to borrow without prior agreement from the federal government. Additionally, most policies implemented by states and municipalities are regulated by federal legislation.

On the other hand, when it comes to the shared rule dimension, the choices made by the framers of the Brazilian constitution were closer to classical federations. There is symmetric bicameralism, senators are elected by parties, and unit representation has a veto power on federal revenue distribution. However, unlike many federations, the Constitution is easier to change, with an average of four amendments per year. So, although constitutional amendment is more difficult as compared to ordinary legislation, an international comparison shows that the Brazilian constitution is easier to change.

That said, the question arises: what is the main divide of the Brazilian federation? There are no divisions like regional identity or ethnic or religion divisions. However, the main divide of the Brazilian Federation is socioeconomic. This can be seen in Figure 1, which displays a map with data on a synthetic indicator of population needs at municipal level, based on 2010 Census data.

Figure 1. Divide between richer and poorer regions (municipalities by synthetic indicator of need, 2010)

Source: IBGE (2012)

Territories in darker tones denote the poorest areas, while those in lighter tones represent the wealthiest. Poverty is concentrated in the north and northeast, whereas the richest regions are in the South and Southeast. The central west region (shown in middle tones) used to align with poorer regions, but recently it has undergone significant changes, becoming very affluent, mainly due to the export of commodities.

Nevertheless, poorer regions outnumber richer ones. This means that a larger number of federal units benefit from arrangements involving transfers from the minority of wealthier regions. Although the number of affluent regions increased (due to the transformations of the center west), richer regions still constitute a minority. As a result, the federal bargain in the Brazilian federation focuses less on subnational autonomy and more on determining the winners and losers in fiscal schemes.

As our fiscal schemes are highly complex, determining winners and losers is not straightforward, and many negotiations occur under a veil of ignorance. The overall outcome of many fiscal bargains is challenging to assess. In any case, shared decisions about cross-regional issues are a key aspect of Brazilian politics. Consequently, the composition and decision-making rules of the Brazilian federation are of utmost importance.

Regarding the composition of federal-level arenas, the key point is how states and municipalities are represented. The table below displays the number of seats each region has in the upper and lower chambers. To continue exploring this topic through the socioeconomic divide, poorer regions are colored in dark gray, while wealthier ones are in light gray. The center west (which can be considered a pivotal region) is colored in medium gray.

Table 2. Distribution of seats by region – Upper and Lower Chambers

REGION	LOWER C	%	UPPER C	%
NORTH	57	11	18	22
NORTHEAST	151	29	27	33
Subtotal	208	41	45	56
CENTER-WEST	49	10	15	19
SOUTH	77	15	9	11
SOUTHEAST	179	35	12	15
Subtotal	256	50	21	26
Total	513	100	81	100

Source: Congresso Nacional (2024)

Many political scientists are critical of the malapportionment formula adopted in Brazil for the allocation of seats. As it stands now, such rules violate the principle of "one man, one vote" in both the lower chamber (house of population) and the upper chamber (Senate or the house of territorial units). However, as originally advanced by Wanderley Guilherme dos Santos, malapportionment in Brazil plays a crucial role in balancing the representation of poorer and richer regions in central decision-making arenas. Poorer states constitute the majority in the upper chamber but the minority in the lower chamber. Conversely, richer states nearly hold a majority in the lower chamber but are a minority in the upper chamber.

Of course, this analysis does not account for political parties, a key aspect that complicates negotiations further. Consider a scenario where one party controls the total number of seats in each region. In such an extreme case, neither richer nor poorer states would be able to form a majority in both houses simultaneously. Therefore, malapportionment, combined with symmetric bicameralism, encourages negotiation among unequal regions regarding federal socioeconomic bargains.

The ongoing changes in the central west region may alter the dynamics of regional negotiations in Brazil, as they affect the composition of regional coalitions. These changes could impact the current balance of regional representation and cross-regional negotiations. We will be able to observe these developments soon.

Let's now turn to the lessons we have learned from our experience with COVID-19. For the sake of simplicity, I would say that we had two strands of orientation regarding fighting COVID. As in many other democracies, we had a negationist faction, which denied science guidance, and a scientific faction. Negationists in Brazil were by no means a small group. Many governors and politicians aligned with this orientation, President Bolsonaro being the leader and the most prominent figure of such a group. Given the central role the Union and the president (as political institutions) have in Brazil, we indeed faced a very, very dangerous and risky situation. Remember that our federation concentrates authority in the Union and our political system concentrates authority in the Presidency.

In March 2020, President Bolsonaro enacted a decree forbidding states and municipalities from making decisions on the mobility of individuals and business activities. By claiming that the Union had exclusive authority on such matters, the President aimed to tie the hands of the opposition, which intended to comply with scientific advice and enforce stay-at-home measures and economic activity slowdowns. So, the federal dispute referred to which level of government had authority to decide on containment measures.

President Bolsonaro's claim was defeated by the Supreme Court, which made a very controversial and unorthodox interpretation of the Brazilian Constitution, siding with scientific expertise. The Court decided that these matters were health-related, so states and municipalities were authorized to make decisions about them. It was a rare event for the Supreme Court not to side with the federal government in disputes involving concurrent powers.

In my interpretation, the Court made an unorthodox interpretation of the Brazilian Constitution allowing states and municipalities to decide on the mobility of individuals. Let's consider this in counterfactual terms. If the judiciary were not independent, President Bolsonaro's preference would have prevailed, likely resulting in even more deaths by COVID. If subnational governments had no capacity to implement health policies, there would have been many more casualties in Brazil. However, the fact that the Ministry of Health was controlled by the negationist group brought about severe coordination problems, precisely because there is multilevel governance in health policy.

Finally, let me briefly address the subject of the role of Brazilian federalism in preventing democratic backsliding. As a result of Bolsonaro's Presidency, the extreme right is much more organized and thus electorally competitive, with no sign of weakening, despite President Lula's victory in the 2022 election.

The independence of the judiciary and the press in Brazil were key elements in guaranteeing the fairness of the competition and ensuring that election results were respected. However, these institutions cannot be solely attributed to federalism. Nevertheless, the simultaneous holding of elections for state governors, state-level assemblies, as well as elections for the lower chamber and the upper chamber on the same day as the presidential election can be considered typical federal institutions that contributed to the respect of the presidential election results. To contest Lula's victory, the extreme right would have been obliged to contest all these elections held on the same day, including those where extreme-right candidates won.

References

Arretche, M. (2015). Intergovernmental relations in Brazil: An unequal federation with symmetrical arrangements. In J. Poirier, C. Saunders, & J. Kincaid (Eds.),

Intergovernmental Relations in Federal Systems (pp. 108-134). Oxford: Oxford University Press.

Arretche, M. (2021). A mutação de Bolsonaro e sua sobrevivência política. *Nexo*, 2024. Retrieved from https://www.nexojornal.com.br/a-mutacao-de-bolsonaro-e-sua-sobrevivencia-politica

Arretche, M., & Lazzari, E. (2023). Reforma tributária de Lula tenta se equilibrar entre correção de distorções e aumento da arrecadação. *Nexo*. Retrieved February 15, 2024, from https://theconversation.com/reforma-tributaria-de-lula-tenta-se-equilibrar-entre-correcao-de-distorcoes-e-aumento-da-arrecadacao-218090

Congresso Nacional. (2024, February 15). Parlamentares em exercício. Retrieved February 15, 2024, from https://www.congressonacional.leg.br/parlamentares/em-exercicio

Hooghe, L. et al. (2016). Measuring Regional Authority: A post-functionalist theory of governance. Oxford: Oxford University Press.

IBGE (Instituto Brasileiro de Geografia e Estatística). (2012). *Censo Brasileiro de 2010*. Rio de Janeiro: IBGE.

Llanos, M. (2003). Los senadores y el senado en Argentina y Brasil: Informe de una encuesta. *Institut Fur Iberoamerika-kunde*. Retrieved February 15, 2024, from https://d-nb.info/970078870/34

Santos, W. G. (1997). Representação, proporcionalidades e democracia. *Estudos Eleitorais*, *1*(1).

4

FEDERALISM, POLITICS IN TIME, AND THE WELFARE STATE AS A CRISIS MANAGER IN THE UNITED STATES AND CANADA

Daniel Béland

Introduction

This chapter explores the interaction between federalism and social policy in times of crisis. As argued below, emergencies are only likely to have a transformative impact on the federalism and social policy nexus when they become a *durable* crisis. In other words, a temporal approach to federalism and social policy development in times of crisis is necessary, and that approach, as shown, must take partisanship (i.e. elections and partisan control) directly into account.

Long-term crises generate cumulative effects that are much more likely to have a transformative political and policy impact than short-term emergencies, a remark consistent with the extensive scholarship on what Paul Pierson (2004) called *Politics in Time*. This is why the temporal aspect of social policy analysis in times of crisis is crucial, leading us to embrace a diachronic approach to the development of policy institutions over time (Jacobs, 2016). This diachronic approach to institutional analysis allows close attention to the time frame used in policy research (Campbell, 2004).

This institutional and temporal approach to crisis and policy change is particularly adapted to federalism, an institutional setting that changes over time (Greer et al., 2023). In this paper, I focus on two federal countries — Canada and the United States — to explore the impact of large-scale economic crises on the role of the federal state in social policy over long time periods. This comparative, temporal, and diachronic approach to the relationship between federalism and "the welfare state as crisis manager" (Starke, Kaasch, & Hooren, 2013) allow us to draw a line between temporary and durable forms of social policy change in the aftermath of economic crises and in the broader yet changing institutional context of federalism.

In this brief chapter, we discuss the politics of federalism and social policy in the United States and Canada during three major economic crises: the Great Depression, the Great Recession that followed the 2008 financial crisis, and the sudden downturn in spring 2020 triggered by the COVID-19 pandemic and the public health restrictions aimed at addressing the spread of the virus. At the beginning of each of these three cases, temporary measures were adopted, often by the federal government but also by some sub-federal units (provinces/territories and states). Yet, in all cases the question is whether these temporary measures translated into permanent policies capable of altering "federal dynamics" over time (Benz & Broschek, 2013).

To assess these effects of large economic crises on the federalism and social policy nexus, this chapter takes a long-term historical and comparative perspective on these two countries and three crises. This analysis should help us better understand how, over time, major crises can set into motion policy changes that are likely to affect federal dynamics and, more specifically, the changing divisions of labour between the federal state and sub-federal units in social policy.

Great Depression

The Great Depression was triggered by the October 1929 financial crash, and it proved particularly long in the United States and Canada. It only ended with the beginning of the Second World War which led to a rapid decline in unemployment, among other things. There were economic ups and downs during the Great Depression but, overall, this economic crisis proved unusually long (Berton, 2012).

From a temporal standpoint, in both the United States and Canada, there was an important lag between the beginning of this economic crisis and the adoption of permanent large-scale federal social programs that altered the federal system over time through the advent of a much more central role of the federal state in social policy. During the Great Depression itself, this was particularly the case in the United States, where the first large permanent federal social programs were only adopted in the mid-1930s (Skocpol, 1992).

To understand this shift, we must turn to partisanship and electoral politics. When the Great Depression hit the country, a Republican president, Herbert Hoover, was in the White House. He was heavily criticized for his lacklustre response to the crisis which helped Democrat Franklin

Delano Roosevelt (FDR) win against him in the 1932 federal elections. In the aftermath of which, Democrats took control of both the House of Representatives and the Senate. This unified Democratic control helped FDR launch and implement his 'New Deal', which dramatically increased the role of the federal state in the U.S. economy.

In terms of social policy, the New Deal was initially dominated by massive, yet temporary public works programs aimed at fighting unemployment (Amenta, 1998). In 1935, however, more than five years after the beginning of the Great Depression, new permanent federal social programs were adopted. A milestone in this area was the signing of the Social Security Act in August 1935. The Social Security Act led to the creation of the first purely federal modern social insurance program. Known today as Social Security, this old-age insurance program survived judicial review by the Supreme Court before playing an instrumental role in the gradual expansion of the federal role in social policy long after the end of the Great Depression, creating a durable centralizing path in U.S. public pension policy (Derthick, 1979). In addition, the Act created grants in aid to the states in the field of social assistance as well as a fiscal and regulatory framework for a decentralized unemployment insurance framework that encouraged states to participate.

In Canada, it took even more time for the permanent expansion of federal social policy to become a reality on the ground. In late 1935, a few months after the signing of the Social Security Act, the government of Canada adopted a centralized unemployment insurance program through the enactment of the Employment and Social Insurance Act. Narrower than the U.S. Social Security Act, this legislation was sponsored by Conservative Prime Minister R.B. Bennett. In the hope to help his party remain in power, his government enacted the piece of legislation just before federal elections, which failed politically as the Liberals won. In contrast to the situation prevailing in the U.S., where the Social Security Act was upheld by the Supreme Court, Canada's unemployment insurance did not survive judicial review, as the Supreme Court of Canada and the London-based Judicial Committee of the Privy Council struck it down on the ground that provincial approval was necessary for the federal government to create such a program. This 1937 judicial turning point forced the federal government to negotiate with the provinces, which further delayed the advent of unemployment insurance in Canada. Ironically, it was only in 1940 that an agreement with the provinces was finalized and that, in the wake of a constitutional amendment, a new unemployment insurance legislation was adopted (Courchene & Allan, 2009) — at a time when unemployment had already decline dramatically due to the beginning of the Second World War the year before.

In Canada as in the United States, the Second World War played a major role in terms of consolidating the role of the federal state in social policy. After the war, however, in Canada there was a pushback against centralization that did not really take place in the United States. Overall, in both countries, the Great Recession and the Second World War led to federal social policy expansion but the preservation of a decentralized framework in a number of key areas of the welfare state (Théret, 2002).

Great Recession

Now, if we move from the Great Depression to the Great Recession to discuss what happened in the aftermath of the 2008 financial crisis in Canada and the United States, temporary measures were enacted in both countries to offer more support for the unemployed, among other things (Béland & Waddan, 2012). Yet, the Great Recession was much shorter than the Great Depression and, for the most part, the temporary measures that were enacted did not last very long. In both the United States and Canada, however, there were some indirect effects of the Great Recession on the social policy agenda and on the debate over increasing the role of the federal government in social policy.

Clearly, in the United States, the debate on what Obamacare would become was already raging before the financial crisis of the fall of 2008. This discourse began during the presidential race between George W. Bush and Barack Obama and helped the latter beat the former at the polls. After the election of Barack Obama, the Great Recession was used as a way to justify the enactment of Obamacare because a lot of people lost their private insurance coverage during the Great Recession. So, in the aftermath of the financial crisis, the Democrats used this situation — the negative consequence of the Great Recession on health insurance coverage—to justify Obamacare. Although it is possible that Obamacare would have been enacted without the Great Recession, it is clear that the Democrats used it to justify this legislation. It also contributed to the increased role of the federal government in health care while triggering a strong negative reaction in

Republican-controlled states, which in turn weakened the implementation of Obamacare over time (Béland, Rocco, & Waddan, 2016).

In Canada, the Great Recession led to a major debate over the potential expansion of the Canada Pension Plan (CPP), which is run by the federal government and covers workers in the three territories and 9 of the 10 provinces, as Quebec opted out of the program to create its own Quebec Pension Plan in the mid-1960s (Bryden, 1974). Within the CPP, the provinces have a veto point in terms of reform, because it is a federal program in which inter-governmental relations are built-in, meaning that the federal government cannot reform it without having support from at least 2/3 of the provinces, representing at least 2/3 of the population (Banting, 2005).

In the immediate aftermath of the financial crisis, pension funds and people's savings were negatively affected, a situation that popularized the idea of increasing the size of public pensions on the left, including and especially the CPP. After the financial crisis, the social-democratic New Democratic Party really put CPP expansion at the centre of its agenda. Yet, the Conservative government of Stephen Harper, which at some point contemplated a potential expansion of CPP, ended up rejecting the idea in response to a push back from their base, particularly from small businesses. Finally, in 2015, the Liberals added CPP expansion to their electoral platform, something particularly important because they did form a majority government after defeating the Conservatives later that year. The expansion of the CPP finally occurred in 2016, after the Liberals took office and found a way to secure a deal over this with the provinces, most of which had a left-of-centre government at the time, which facilitated intergovernmental cooperation (Béland & Weaver, 2019).

Overall, for partisan and electoral reasons, CPP expansion only took place nearly six years after the onset of the Great Recession, but it did set this debate and agenda-setting process into motion. In this context we can say that, in Canada, the Great Recession had an indirect effect on CPP expansion, just like it had an indirect effect on the politics of Obamacare in the United Stares. In both countries, the interaction between the timing of the crisis and partisan/politics also proved striking, as both Obamacare and CPP expansion were enacted not long after elections leading to a partisan change in government.

COVID-19

In the United Stares and Canada, the COVID-19 pandemic and the public health restrictions it triggered led to a sudden and most dramatic economic downfall, as the unemployment rate increased dramatically in late March and early April 2020. This sudden economic crisis led the federal state in both countries to enact massive, yet temporary, programs. This was a form of deficit spending on a large scale to send money to people who had lost income, or even to people in general, so that they could keep consuming and the economy could stay afloat. It allowed people to cope with this very difficult and unusual economic situation (Béland, Dinan, Rocco, & Waddan, 2021).

Consequently, many of the temporary measures that were enacted to support families, the unemployed, and people who had lost income during the beginning of the pandemic were lifted and dismantled over time. In terms of *permanent* social policy, in Canada, there were some indirect effects of the pandemic in terms of bringing about an electoral alliance between the NDP and the Liberals. This 'supply-and-confidence' agreement was formalized in March 2022 with the signing of a legislative agreement between the two parties to prompt the minority Liberal government of Justin Trudeau. This agreement helped foster federal social policy expansion in the area of dental care (Béland & Massé, 2023). In the United States, there was an attempt to make temporary child benefits permanent after Joe Biden replaced Donald Trump in the White House in the aftermath of the 2020 presidential elections, but these efforts failed (Béland, Dinan, Rocco, & Waddan, 2022). At the same time, the economic downturn was short-lived. The economy started to recover even in mid-to-late 2020.

Overall, the impact of the COVID-19 pandemic on social policy, in terms of its permanent effects on federalism and social policy, has been limited so far, especially in the United States, which had a Republican president when the crisis hit the country. Yet, it might still be too early to understand the long-term indirect effects of such a recent crisis, which can take years to materialize, a remark that stresses once again the temporal nature of policy change and the need to pay close attention to the time frame used to analyse it over time (Campbell, 2004).

Discussion: The Time Frame and the Evolution of Partisanship

If you look at the United States and Canada, these three crises — the Great Depression, the Great Recession, and the recent COVID-19 crisis — all increased the social policy role of the federal government, at least temporarily. Yet, in terms of permanent reforms, the Great Depression had the largest effect over time, partly because it simply lasted longer. It was a very long crisis and it also started before the advent of the modern welfare state, a situation that made that crisis a greater source of economic security than the two more recent crises, which occurred after large social programs had been created, thus making the creation of new permanent programs less necessary, at least in the short run. This is the case simply because policy legacies build over time and that responses to each new crisis takes place in an environment structured by previous welfare state expansion triggered in part by earlier crises (Pierson, 1996). Simultaneously, compared to the Great Depression, the two other crises under investigation, especially the COVID-19 economic crisis, were relatively short-lived, and their effects were overall more temporary than permanent.

The duration of the crisis in the context of existing policy legacies is an important fact to understand the impact of major crises on federalism and social policy development. Yet, as suggested above, partisanship as it relates to electoral outcomes is another key factor here. For example, in Canada the expansion of CPP in the aftermath of the Great Depression only became possible because of a major partisan realignment when the Conservatives of Stephen Harper were defeated by the Liberals of Justin Trudeau in the fall of 2015. This example illustrates the importance of change in partisan control over time, which once again points to the importance of the time frame used for the analysis of change in both federalism and social policy, especially with regard to the indirect effects of crises. As for partisanship, we cannot understand its influence because, as the cases of both Obamacare and CPP expansion, it matters a great deal to know what political parties support and which of them is in power and when at the federal level, but also at the sub-federal level. The role of sub-federal governments was not discussed in this chapter because my time was limited.

The above analysis is very short and a lot more could be said about the three crises briefly discussed above, as far as their impact of federalism and social policy is concerned. Yet, this analysis does suggest a way forward for future research on the topic. What we need is a fine-grained process tracing approach that recognizes the importance of temporality and the timeframe of the analysis, in terms of policy effects and legacies as well as changing partisan control and orientations. Clearly, if you look at the impact of a crisis on federalism and social policy over just six months, a year, or even two or three years, scholars might miss important institutional and policy effects that have yet to materialize. This is why a long-term approach to crises, federalism, and social policy and how they interact remains imperative moving forward.

Acknowledgements

This chapter is derived from a presentation delivered remotely on July 24, 2023, at the International Seminar on Federalism and Democracy in an Era of Emergencies (São Paulo). The author thanks Alan Fenna and the other participants for their comments and suggestions as well as Ally Hays-Alberstat for the editorial support.

References

Amenta, E. (1998). *Bold relief: Institutional politics and the origins of modern American social policy*. Princeton: Princeton University Press.

Banting, K. G. (2005). Canada: Nation-building in a federal welfare state. In H. Obinger, L. S. Leibfried, & F. G. Castles (Eds.), *Federalism and the welfare state: New world and European experiences* (pp. 89-137). Cambridge: Cambridge University Press.

Béland, D., Dinan, S., Rocco, P., & Waddan, A. (2022). COVID-19, poverty reduction, and partisanship in Canada and the United States. *Policy and Society*, 41(2), 291-305.

Béland, D., Dinan, S., Rocco, P., & Waddan, A. (2021). Social policy responses to COVID-19 in Canada and the United States: Explaining policy variations between two liberal welfare state regimes. *Social Policy & Administration*, 55(2), 280-294.

Béland, D., & Massé, L. (2023, December 28). Is the supply-and-confidence deal between the Liberals and NDP on life support? The Conversation. Retrieved from https://theconversation.com/will-the-supply-and-confidence-deal-between-the-liberals-and-ndp-survive-in-2024-219478

Béland, D., Rocco, P., & Waddan, A. (2016). *Obamacare Wars: Federalism, State Politics, and the Affordable Care Act*. Kansas City: University Press of Kansas.

Béland, D., & Waddan, A. (2012). The great recession and US social policy: From expansion to austerity. In M. Kilkey, G. Ramia, & K. Farnsworth (Eds.), *Social Policy Review 24: Analysis and Debate in Social Policy* (pp. 277-296). Policy Press.

Béland, D., & Weaver, R. K. (2019). Federalism and the politics of the Canada and Quebec pension plans. *Journal of International and Comparative Social Policy*, 35(1), 25-40.

Benz, A., & Broschek, J. (Eds.). (2013). *Federal dynamics: Continuity, change, and varieties of federalism*. Oxford: Oxford University Press.

Berton, P. (2012). *The great depression, 1929-1939*. Toronto: Doubleday Canada.

Bryden, K. (1974). *Old age pensions and policy-making in Canada*. Montreal: McGill-Queen's University Press.

Campbell, J. L. (2004). *Institutional change and globalization*. Princeton: Princeton University Press.

Courchene, T. J., & Allan, J. R. (2009). A short history of EI and a look at the road ahead. *Policy Options*, 19-28.

Derthick, M. (1979). *Policymaking for social security*. Washington, DC: Brookings Institution.

Greer, S. L. et al. (2023). Putting federalism in place: *The territorial politics of social policy revisited*. Chicago: University of Michigan Press.

Jacobs, A. M. (2016). Social policy dynamics. In O. Fioretos, T. G. Falleti, & A. Sheingate (Eds.), *The Oxford handbook of historical institutionalism* (pp. 142-162). Oxford: Oxford University Press.

Pierson, P. (2004). Politics in time: History, institutions, and social analysis. Princeton: Princeton University Press.

Pierson, P. (1996). The new politics of the welfare state. World Politics, 48(1), 143-179.

Skocpol, T. (1992). Protecting soldiers and mothers: The political origins of social policy in the United States. Harvard: The Belknap Press of Harvard University Press.

Starke, P., Kaasch, A., & Hooren, F. (2013). *The welfare state as crisis manager: Explaining the diversity of policy responses to economic crisis*. London: Palgrave.

Théret, B. (2002). *Protection sociale et fédéralisme: L'Europe dans le miroir de l'Amérique du Nord*. Montreal: Presses de l'Université de Montréal.

FEDERALISM AND DEMOCRACY: CONNECTIONS AND CHALLENGES

Jared Sonnicksen

Introduction

Federalism and democracy are interlinked and interrelated in many ways. From a theoretical standpoint, they share several basic constitutional-political principles which are connected, for instance, to division of powers, equality of constituents, and self-government. However, the reference points of these principles differ, with democracy oriented more toward self-governing 'peoples' and federalism toward self-governing 'places'. Thus, the interconnections between federalism and democracy raise particular challenges already in theory and principle (see for overview Sonnicksen, 2018). These challenges arise in practices of government too, not least in cases of crises, emergencies, or other problems that cross jurisdictions and levels of government. Thus, whether federalism is good for democracy, whether democracy is good for federalism, and whether one or both together are good at dealing with policy challenges in general and emergency situations in particular – these questions are each on their own difficult to answer, and form together a veritable dilemma.

Thus, it is unsurprising that federalism and democracy are in a complex relationship, and that this relationship can become additionally complicated in times of crises, and surely in an era of emergencies. The ongoing climate crisis and its looming exacerbation have long posed a cross-border challenge and a 'super wicked problem' par excellence, since it confronts all societies and levels of government, which at the same time are endowed with territorially and politically delimited jurisdictions and respectively restricted scopes of competences (Kemmerzell, 2019). However, with the COVID-19 pandemic, comparably profound challenges – from unequal and uneven resource distribution, to mismatches between problems and problem-solving capacities – became even more salient and palpable. The world has faced a problem that truly affected the *pandemos* or all people, with immediately tangible effects in numerous areas of life. Moreover, like the climate crisis, the Coronavirus pandemic could not be solved per se, but only dealt and coped with, and this in parallel in different countries and, within them, in different constituencies. There is no *pantopos* or all-encompassing 'place' (e.g. global super-state, planetary government, or similar) to commensurately 'match' and address the pandemic-problem.

Furthermore, how the different political systems are configured or organized, in turn, affects how a cross-cutting problem like a pandemic is dealt with or addressed, and even perceived or defined in the first place. As such, the question becomes not only how do federal democracies deal with a crisis, but also what does a federal democratic system do to a crisis. Taking the extreme case of the pandemic as an emergency that affects all people and knows no borders or constituencies, nevertheless, there is no world to address it. Instead, a world of states transforms a problem into different 'national' ones. In the federal democracies, moreover, it becomes an issue that must be grappled with by different governments at different levels and of the different constituent units, e.g. of Sao Paulo and Minas Gerais, of Bremen and North-Rhine Westphalia, of Alaska and Vermont, and so forth. In other words, and at latest visible in an era of emergencies and of unbounded challenges, all or most politics may still be local, not because the problems but rather the polities are.

Consequently, federalism does something to a crisis – and many policy issues – in transforming it through the federal territorial-political organization of states or polities, for instance triggering also such questions of which level is responsible. Similar goes for the democratic-governmental dimension of the polity, which links governance to requisites of popular rule, such as representativeness, responsiveness and responsibility to the people. These federal and democratic concerns evoke obviously two quite different questions – e.g. in short: which level of government is responsible (federal), which solution or option do (most) people prefer (democratic) – to address than merely the question of how to solve a problem.

There is no clear-cut answer as to whether federal and democratic principles compel different people and places to resolve common problems together or to go their separate ways, whether in the interest of democracy, of federalism, of pluralism or policy-experimentalism, among others. At the same time, issues of equality, welfare and vulnerability or resilience may require precisely equalization, coordination and variegated means and mechanisms for managing inequalities and interdependencies. These concerns related to profound human vulnerability (Fineman, 2021), especially in an era of emergencies, invite perhaps reflecting again on federal democracy, with a view more toward shared rule and cooperation rather than self-rule, autonomy, and unilateralism. The crises and emergencies of recent years warrant renewed consideration of what holds political communities together, in general, and what can help federal democracies work and to maintain a balance between self- and shared rule in particular.

Against this backdrop, the following briefly sketches the complexity of connections and challenges of a federal democracy. While the preceding remarks provide already an overview, it is worth revisiting federalism and democracy in a first step. Then, the contribution elaborates on what connects and what challenges them especially in practices of governance. Finally, it concludes with a further, albeit preliminary, reflection on emergencies and vulnerability and their implications for a viable federal democracy.

Distinguishing Federalism and Democracy

Politics in general can be conceived to have a fundamental interconnection with several basic parameters, or analogously, cardinal directions, but which take on a special relevance for federalism and democracy. I summarize them in own compact fashion as dimensions or directions of the polity as an institutionalized political community, namely *power*, *principles*, *people* and *places* (see figure 1 below).

Figure 1. A Simple Cartography of the Political Landscape

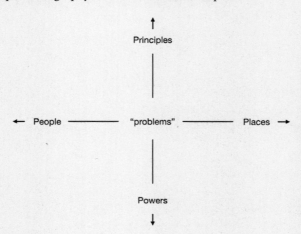

Source: Own depiction

With a view to this simplified mapping, any modern political community faces collective policy as well as many other political problems that must be addressed in a multidimensional context. That is to say, there is the dimension of *powers* (including rights and responsibilities or restrictions) and how they are distributed to which actors or institutions. *Places* refer to the space or delimited body politic and territory in which politics transpires. Other kinds of boundaries refer to the *people* themselves who are e.g. affected by the issue and are to be addressed and/or subjected to a political decision. All of this interlinks with a dimension of *principles*, including constitutional ones, various values, norms, and further ideas that frame, guide or co-influence political contestation. In a federal democracy – as opposed to, say, a unitary autocracy – these dimensions or 'cardinal directions' of the political space each become more complex.

Political authority or sovereignty in modern polities – of course not only but typically institutionalized in a state – is bound as a rule to a delimited territory and a people or population. The democratic constitution of the polity populates that space with a multitude of citizens supposed to be equal. A federal system multiplies this space further with constituent units – whether named *estados*, provinces, *Länder*, states etc. – endowed with constitutional authority. Both democratic people and federal places represent thus *pouvoir constituants* (Hueglin, 2023). Hence, federalism and democracy have much in common as organizing principles of government. They involve extensive distributions of power that are grounded in notions of liberty and equality as well as collective self-government, all of which is typically further underpinned by a constitution.

Figure 2. Common Features of Democracy and Federalism

Features	Democracy	Federalism
Constitution	Demos	Foedus
Division of powers	Branches of government	Levels of government
Constituency	Citizens	Constituent units (e.g. states, regions)
Equality		
Representation	Population-, group-based	Territory/region-based

Source: Own depiction

At the same time, they are distinct dimensions of government that have different points of reference and that follow different logics of operation (see figure 2 above). These circumstances are not merely a self-evident matter, since federalism and democracy were long thought to be mutually compatible and even reinforcing. However, neither federalism nor democracy is internally monolithic. Both have various models and subtypes, while the relationship between them turns out to be much more complex and laden with tensions (see e.g. Benz & Sonnicksen, 2017; Stepan, 1999). Again, these tensions derive in part from mutuality in principles like divided authority and equality. Yet, they do not always coincide and can stand at odds on account of different reference points and logics of governance.

Democratic models, in conventional representative government alone, range from more majority oriented and power concentrating to more power diffusing and consensus oriented (see e.g. Liphart, 2012). Similar may be surmised regarding conventional federal systems, ranging from more power separating and dualistic between the levels of government to more power sharing and cooperating in character (Watts, 2008; see also the chapter by Alana Fenna in this volume). By dividing power across levels and constituent units, federalism may comparatively multiply the spaces and places of democratic participation (see e.g. Fraenkel, Kropp, Palermo & Sommermann, 2015; Kropp, 2015). Federalism in turn could be expected to strengthen democracy for these reasons, while democracy may be expected to stabilize federalism. Both government dimensions divide, instead of concentrating, powers among branches (democracy) and levels (federalism) of government, and thus essentially among the people(s). Nevertheless, the two follow different organizational principles.

Democracy has a constituent multitude, while there are manifold constituent governments in federalism. The latter comprises an intergovernmental relationship between levels of government vertically as well as horizontally among the constituent units. The former entails a division of power among the citizens and between branches of government. These comprise the institutional default settings of a federal democracy. Again, however, there are also different variants of each of these dimensions that may end up combined in one polity: e.g. a presidential democracy with a dual federal system, or a parliamentary democracy with a cooperative federal system, and so forth. This combination does not necessarily lead to a particular kind or a certain quality of policy outcomes or levels of citizen support (Arretche, Schlegel, & Ferrari, 2016; Obinger, Leibfried, & Castles,

2005; Wachendorfer-Schmidt, 2000), but it does foster different patterns of politics (see e.g. Benz & Sonnicksen, 2021). For instance, a dual federal system by constitutional predisposition may drift more toward cooperative federalism. A parliamentary system may evolve though intergovernmental conferences among ministers that remain dependent on their parliamentary majorities in parliament. A presidential system could bring forth networks of coordination connecting the legislatures and administrations in federal practice. In any case, there are different types of combinations of democratic systems and of federal systems. Moreover, how they are combined matters for how they operate in practice.

Connecting Federalism and Democracy in Governance

The relationship between federalism and democracy is actually one of many different relationships. This claim applies, also because there are different models of federalism combined with different models of democracy, and there may be different patterns that emerge even within individual cases (Benz & Sonnicksen, 2021; cf. on the Brazilian case Grin & Abrucio, 2021). Democracy in a federative setting affects federalism at work since the 'internal logics' of federalism are affected by how the democratic governments are configured. The same goes for federalism having effect on democratic government, from whether and how elected governments can decide and implement policy, to the organization of the political party system, among many others. From the outset, moreover, a federal democracy sets multiple dimensions, bounds and boundaries for the polity, its political decision and policymaking. This combination of two different kinds of dimensions of government comes with challenges that apply to everyday governance. They may intensify in times of particularly difficult challenges, emergencies or crises and especially those transcending or crossing jurisdictions and affecting multiple regions or the polity as a whole. One such basic challenge refers to incongruencies or mismatches between the distribution of power and resources on the one hand, and an actual problem to be addressed, on the other. The latter may not – and often does not – match neatly with jurisdiction or scope of powers and/or the effective capacity to deal with the problem.

With the democratic dimension of government alone, interactions and coordination can take many forms and modes between branches of government in order to come to agreements, for instance through negotiations, coalition talks (particularly in parliamentary democracies), informal ongoing dialogues, and more. In the federal dimension, the spectrum may be said to run from more separation of powers to sharing of powers, between self- and shared rule (Elazar, 1987). Ultimately though, one may say that federalism is fundamentally about shared rule. The very character of federalism lies not only in separation and divided authority – if that were the case, the constituent units need not bother joining or being part of a federation – but rather finding some kinds and degrees of cooperation and coordination, not least in a democratic polity (Mueller, 2019). Similar applies to democratic governance. It cannot operate by strict adherence to separation of powers and branches alone, but always necessitates cross-branch interactions and ultimately consensus-seeking and agreements in order to operate at all.

Accordingly, and perhaps thus unsurprisingly, intergovernmental relations make up part and parcel of any modern federal democracy. Again though, these relations manifest with quite variable forms in different federal democracies, from informal to more formal and institutionalized patterns, from networks and lobbying to more routinized administrative and ministerial conferences, among others (Bolleyer, 2006; Schnabel, 2020). However, institutions and practices of intergovernmental cooperation and coordination, irrespective of how well organized or institutionalized they are, do not guarantee that federal democracies adequately manage their interdependencies or resolve cross-jurisdictional problems and tasks. To do so requires ongoing commitments and efforts. They are not easy, and often stand in tension or at odds with democratic mandates and rules of the game or with the strict federal distribution of powers.

Conclusion

What follows from all of the above is that federalism and democracy are complex, if anything simply because they are multidimensional. This also means that a federal democracy has complex government as its institutional default settings thanks to its constitutional organization of government. However, this also implicates that a federal democracy has – indeed requires – complex government and governance in practice. Such governance necessitates processes of relationships and interactions between multiple branches and multiple levels of government, not to mention also with various collective actors, groups and sectors of society.

Most modern problems are not strictly local ones. And even those that are rather locally concentrated, decisions dealing with them can have effects that cross territories. Thus, they can create externalities for other communities as well as trigger or intensify interdependencies. Sometimes federalism is treated as a kind of democratic response to diversity. Or it may be a democratic response to conflict. But actually, federalism is also a conflict transformation. Political contestation never ends. Federalism and democracy offer a way of managing contestation and hopefully pacifying conflicts. At the same time, the federal character of a polity and democratic dynamics can also create new kinds of conflicts and certainly externalities through policy making.

Finally, and consequently, many modern political problems are complex and territorially, though also temporally, unbounded. They have required adaptations of federal democracy specifically toward more cooperative oriented relationships in order to manage these governance challenges – from welfare to modern regulatory state, environmental protection, disaster management, public health, and much more. Given these ongoing challenges, but also in the light of the pandemic and other crises at latest, it would appear that cooperation and coordination belong to the most pressing and fundamental tasks of a federal democracy. The pandemic revealed in superlative, almost omnipresent ways, that vulnerability lies at the base of the human condition both individually and collectively (cf. again also Fineman, 2021). The era of emergencies may heighten this awareness too. This does and should not mean the political imperatives of a state of emergency that could undermine broad power sharing or the protection of pluralism. On the contrary, the challenge of a federal democracy more than ever calls for striking a balance between self-rule and shared rule (Elazar, 1987) and between autonomy and interdependence (Benz, 2020). Finally, this also means embracing federalism and democracy not only as conditions or sets of formal institutions and structures, but also and especially as processes in order to make federal democracy work.

References

Arretche, M., Schlegel, R., & Ferrari, D. (2016). Preferences regarding the vertical distribution of authority in Brazil: On measurements and determinants. *Publius, 46*(1), 77-107.

Benz, A. (2020). *Föderale Demokratie: Regieren im Spannungsfeld von Interdependenz und Autonomie*. Baden-Baden: Nomos.

Benz, A., & Sonnicksen, J. (2017). Patterns of federal democracy: Tensions, friction, or balance between two government dimensions. *European Political Science Review, 9*(1), 3-25.

Benz, A., & Sonnicksen, J. (Eds.). (2021). *Federal democracies at work: Varieties of complex government*. Toronto: University of Toronto Press.

Bolleyer, N. (2006). Federal dynamics in Canada, the United States, and Switzerland: How substates' internal organization affects intergovernmental relations. *Publius, 36*(4), 471-502.

Elazar, D. J. (1987). *Exploring federalism*. Tuscaloosa: University of Alabama Press.

Fineman, M. (2021). Populations, pandemics, and politics. *International Journal of Discrimination and the Law, 21*(3), 184-190.

Fraenkel-Haeberle, C., Kropp, S., Palermo, F., & Sommermann, K. (Eds.). (2015). *Citizen participation in multi-level democracies*. Leiden: Brill.

Grin, E. J., & Abrucio, F. L. (2021). Hybridism as a national policy style: Paths and dilemmas of the majoritarian and consensus approaches in Brazil. *Revista Brasileira de Ciência Política, 35*, 1-59.

Hueglin, T. (2023). Federalism: From constitutionalism to constitutionalization. In A. Lang, & A. Wiener (Eds.), *Handbook on global constitutionalism* (2nd ed., pp. 448-459). Cheltenham: Edward Elgar.

Hueglin, T., & Fenna, A. (2015). *Comparative federalism: A systematic inquiry* (2nd ed.). Toronto: University of Toronto Press.

Kemmerzell, J. (2019). Bridging the gap between the local and the global scale? Taming the wicked problem of climate change through trans-local governance. In N. Behnke, J. Broschek, & J. Sonnicksen (Eds.), *Configurations, dynamics and mechanisms of multilevel governance* (pp. 155-172). Cham: Palgrave Macmillan.

Kropp, S. (2015). Federalism, people's legislation, and associative democracy. In C. Fraenkel-Haeberle, S. Kropp, F. Palermo, & K. Sommermann (Eds.), *Citizen participation in multi-level democracies* (pp. 48-66). Leiden: Brill.

Lijphart, A. (2012). *Patterns of democracy: Government forms and performance in thirty-six countries* (2nd ed.). New Haven: Yale University Press.

Mueller, S. (2019). Federalism and the politics of shared rule. In J. Kincaid (Ed.), *A research agenda for federalism studies* (pp. 162-174). Cheltenham: Edward Elgar.

Obinger, H., Leibfried, S., & Castles, F. (Eds.). (2005). *Federalism and the welfare state: New world and European experiences.* Cambridge: Cambridge University Press.

Schnabel, J. (2020). *Managing interdependencies in federal systems: Intergovernmental councils and the making of public policy.* Cham: Palgrave Macmillan.

Sonnicksen, J. (2018). Federalism and democracy: A tense relationship. In J. Tudela, M. Kölling, & F. Reviriego (Eds.), *Calidad democrática y organización territorial* (pp. 31–52). Madrid: Marcial Pons.

Stepan, A. (1999). Federalism and democracy: Beyond the U.S. model. *Journal of Democracy, 10*(4), 19-34.

Wachendorfer-Schmidt, U. (Ed.). (2000). *Federalism and political performance.* London: Routledge.

Watts, R. (2008). *Comparing federal systems* (3rd ed.). Montreal: McGill-Queen's University Press.

6

FEDERALISM AND DEMOCRACY IN CONTEMPORARY FEDERALISM: OVERCOMING A LONG TRAJECTORY OF DECOUPLING AND CREATING NEW FORMS OF COUPLING

Fernando Luiz Abrucio

Introduction

Federalism and Democracy are the two main institutional pillars of contemporary Brazilian democracy, with a marriage that has never been as strong as it is today. However, this relationship has been complicated, if not absent, throughout most of Brazil's history. Only in the last thirty years has a more effective link been built between the Federation and the democratic regime. What caused this phenomenon? What are its characteristics? And what lessons can the Brazilian experience bring to the comparative debate? To answer these questions, the chapter analyzes this new and unprecedented coupling between federalism and democracy in Brazilian history. The objective is to highlight the main forms of mutual strengthening derived from this combination. The chapter's structure is as follows.

In the first part, the conceptual debate on the possible connections between federalism and democracy is summarized. The main point here is to show that federative models differ around the world not only because they have different institutional structures, but because throughout the trajectory of each country there have been various types of interlinkages between democratic politics and the federal arrangement. The Brazilian case illustrates this argument because, throughout history, there have been moments of absence of both federalism and democracy, periods of decoupling between the two, fragile connections and, since 1988, a growing strengthening of the coupling between federalism and democracy, even though there are still institutional cracks and weaknesses.

The second part of the article provides a brief description of the historical trajectory of the connection between federalism and democracy in Brazil. For most of Brazilian history, there was weak coupling, or almost none, between the federative model and the democratic regime. However, this does not mean that the political-territorial issue was not important for the political system. Federalism has been constitutionally present since 1891 and was only abolished for a short period of time (1937-1945). Both authoritarian and democratic periods have always had the federative issue as a central theme in Brazilian politics (Abrucio, 1998; Samuels & Abrucio, 2000; Hagopian, 1996). The most important aspect of this work is the discussion on Brazilian redemocratization, which led to an unprecedented and significant strengthening of the ties between federalism and democracy.

Firstly, we briefly discuss the conditions that facilitated this closer connection. Subsequently, the successes and limitations of the coupling between federalism and democracy in Brazil are presented, analyzing a historical process that began with the 1988 federal Constitution and that developed incrementally over approximately thirty years. The ultimate test of this model was the Bolsonaro Government (2019-2022), led by a far-right populist president who favored neither the Federation nor the democratic regime. At the end, the chapter highlights how the characteristics of the Brazilian case can be interconnected with the conceptual and comparative debate on the connection between federalism and democracy.

The various types and paths of the marriage between Federalism and Democracy: conceptual proposal

There is no inherent relationship between federalism and democracy, but there are many affinities and potentialities in their combination. This conceptual debate can be schematically divided into two main lines of argument. The first is related to a broad literature on how the federative model is intrinsically linked to a democratic regime. This represents an older and more lasting tradition of arguments, which initially stems from the liberal matrix of The Federalists Papers and was later developed more fully by authors such as Dahl (1986), Elazar (1987) and Stepan (1999).

More recently, however, there has been a growing literature that focuses on the tensions and difficulties of this marriage (Benz & Sonnicksen, 2015; Sonnicksen, 2018). The ambivalences and mismatches mainly concern the differences between the types of federalism and democracy, and how such institutional combinations in each context are very complex. As Sonnicksen (2024) rightly argues, federalism and democracy, despite having affinities, are different institutional phenomena. Democracy is related to popular sovereignty and division of Powers. Federalism concerns a territorial pact of power (*Foedus*), aimed at ensuring autonomy for levels of government and creating mechanisms of interdependence between federative territorial entities (self-rule plus shared rule). The principles of equality and freedom among citizens helped strengthen Federations, just as the vertical division of power between governments can prevent tyranny (in James Madison's terms), and decentralization can generate greater ability for voters to hold governments accountable.

The interlinkage between federalism and democracy, however, does not always result in positive gains for both sides. The federative model can, for example, generate the need for so much intergovernmental consensus that it can generate democratic decision-making paralysis, as shown by Fritz Sharpf (1988) in his study of the German case. In institutional terms, perhaps the greatest example of inconsistency between federalism and democracy is the Electoral College that defines American presidential elections. Created to guarantee greater equality between federative entities, the Electoral College today has the power to distort the majority principle that guides the democratic ideal (Dahl, 2001; Keyssar, 2020). Understanding the complexity of the link between federalism and democracy is also important to avoid an evolutionist and, at times, colonialist comparative analysis. In fact, the consolidation of democracy and its coupling with federative logic has been very complicated in Federations located in Latin America, Africa and Asia. This is undeniable. Despite this, studies have increasingly shown the tensions and difficulties of older Federations and/or developed countries in successfully combining the principles of ***demos*** (pact between individuals) and *foedus* (pact between territories).

This paper proposes that to avoid a mere evolutionist view in comparative federalism, it is necessary to add three more arguments to this debate. The first is about the effect of the multiplicity of situations of territorial heterogeneity, from the point of view of the weight and meaning of the diversities existing in each Federation, and the way in which they evolve historically. The second concerns how other political process affect the articulation between federalism and democracy. And the third point is the development of Sonnicksen's (2018; 2024) idea that it is necessary to think about degrees of coupling between federalism and democracy.

The connection between federalism and democracy depends largely on how the territorial heterogeneities of federal countries are resolved by a political model that seeks to guarantee unity in diversity. Federations arise in countries where there is relevant territorial heterogeneity, which generates the need for a special power pact to build the nation and define its governance (Burgess, 1993).

In this sense, there are several types of diversity present in federal countries: ethnic, linguistic, religious, different political formations and world views of local elites, socioeconomic inequalities between regions, strong geographic contrasts. In terms classically defined by Burgess, the question is how to guarantee national unity and, at the same time, protect diversity, especially that which manifests itself territorially. It is from this perspective that the idea of a necessary marriage between federalism and democracy emerges. The weight of the constituent heterogeneities of each Federation varies greatly. This has a major effect on democracy because the issue (or issues) that are most important for each *foedus* can be more or less complex to be addressed by the political system.

In the Brazilian case, territorial inequality has become central as a structural diversity of federalism and its resolution is not simple for a middle-income country, territorially extensive and with a large population. It is necessary to add this argument to the comparative debate about the interconnection between federalism and democracy: the weight of more structural territorial heterogeneity (or heterogeneities) affects the democratic capacity to deal with the objective of creating unity in diversity. It is also important to emphasize that this territorial issue transforms over time, and such historical changes relate to changes in the political system. To avoid an overly evolutionist comparison, the debate must incorporate a vision of historical neo-institutionalism that captures the temporal dynamics between and within each Federation (Benz & Broschek, 2013; Broschek, Petereson, & Toubeau, 2017). A second argument must be included to guide the discussion about the relationship between federalism and democracy. In addition to broader institutional differences, such as the contrast between majority and consensual democracy or between government systems, it is necessary to incorporate central themes into the public agenda that affect the governance of countries – and, by extension, the coupling between federalism and democracy.

The Brazilian case illustrates this point well. The joint strengthening of federalism and democracy in Brazil was driven by three issues that gained centrality on the public agenda following redemocratization: a broad expansion of the Welfare State, the construction of a stronger system of checks and balances and the pressure for greater citizen participation. All these issues not only strengthened the Federation and the democratic regime, but also increased the coupling between them. One a more general level, the role of the main political leaders who command the Federation also makes a difference. When Presidents Trump and Bolsonaro acted against state and local governments during COVID-19, they undermined the idea of a more democratic federalism, while leaders in Germany and Canada did just the opposite, strengthening federal ties and democracy itself (Peters, Grin, & Abrucio, 2021). Comparative studies on the relationship between Federations and democratic regimes, finally, need to escape the dualist model. Sonnicksen's (2018; 2024) seminal proposal on coupling gradations between federalism and democracy is essential to better understand the complexity and uniqueness of federative experiences – using categories such as decoupling and coupling (loosing coupling and tightly coupling). A perspective that is based on a combination scale is also better suited to capturing the historical dynamics of each case.

The analysis of the trajectory and recent transformations that have occurred in Brazil will use the inspiration of Sonnicksen's model. It is a country that originally did not have coupled federalism or democracy, but today it has created different forms of coupling, although there are still fissures and weaknesses in this relationship.

Brief History of Absence and Decoupling: The Brazilian case

Brazil became independent in 1822 and adopted a unitary form of State, which persisted for almost 70 years. Thus, in its early stages, the Brazilian model was neither federative nor democratic. Instead, a parliamentary monarchical system was adopted, granting the Emperor significant power, with minimal institutional oversight, and imposing substantial barriers to full citizenship – only 5% of the people voted regularly. The beginning of Brazil's independent trajectory was one of absence of federalism and democracy, and not of decoupling of both. Nonetheless, there were latent territorial heterogeneities. They were linked to geographic issues (large territorial extension, with different parts of the country very far from the control of the center of power), cultural regionalism (very diverse customs and accents) and, mainly, the demand for self-government on the part of different elites and provincial communities. The presence of constitutive territorial heterogeneities is a characteristic that determines the existence of a federative problem, even if there is no Federation. Anyway, the existence of a latent federalism in the Brazilian Empire put national unity at risk. Proof of this is that Brazil went through several local revolts in the 1830s and 1840s, which almost led to secession processes. After this period of civil wars spread across the nation, a strongly centralized model was adopted. The strongly centralized model was long-lasting but resulted in great tension between the Central Government and provincial elites. These elites only tolerated this loss of political power because the Emperor upheld slavery.

However, with the abolition of slavery, local oligarchies stopped supporting the monarchy and actively worked to proclaim the Republic, alongside the military (Carvalho, 2012). The fact is that the political class worked to end the monarchical model to build a federalism designed basically to decentralize power to the "barons". In this context, Republic and Federalism were born uncoupled from democracy in Brazil. The period from 1889 to 1930 was characterized by centrifugal federalism, with great state autonomy, weak local governments, and a Federal Government with few instruments for national action. This type of Federation favored the maintenance of regional oligarchies based on single state parties. Governors are the key part of the political system, both internally within the states because there was very little institutional control over them, and externally because the alliances between them, especially among the richest and/or most populous states, defined presidential candidacies (Abrucio, 1998). Electoral fraud was the hallmark of the political system. Brazil's initial federalism was dissociated from democracy and increased regional inequality.

At the end of this historical period, pressure increased against the oligarchic model in favor of strengthening central power. As a result of this political movement, Getulio Vargas led a revolution in 1930, and assumed power with the proposal of greater political centralization and an expansion of the State's role in the economy. The Vargas vision of the State built a modern Brazilian State. He established the Weberian pillars of federal public administration and boosted national capitalism, fostering conditions for industrialization, urbanization and national integration in a country that was still highly fragmented. However, this entire modernization process was achieved at the cost of weakening federalism and through an autocratic model. Vargas was in power for 15 years (1930-1945), and between 1937 and 1945 the Federation was formally extinguished by the Constitution. In a nutshell, a centralizing and authoritarian model was established. With the deposition of Vargas, Brazil experienced, between 1946 and 1964, a period of coupling federalism with democracy for the first time. States regained their autonomy and regular elections were held at all levels of government.

However, it can be argued that both the quality of the Federation and the democratic regime were still incipient, as was the coupling between them. The culmination of this double fragility was the dismissal of João Goulart from the Presidency of the Republic in 1964, through an alliance between the military and some governors, who collaborated to dismantle the democratic regime. The 1964 military coup generated an authoritarian regime that lasted 20 years. In order to remain in power for so long, the military reduced all political and social controls to the maximum. Parties were extinguished, freedom of expression was censored, and opponents of the regime were arrested, with several of them tortured and killed. One of the main authoritarian instruments was the reduction of the autonomy of state governments, making elections for governor indirect. The purpose of this was to weaken vertical checks and balances over the Union (Sallum Jr., 1996; Abrucio, 1998).

In few words, federalism and democracy are enemies of the military regime. Although some elections were held, they were kept under tight control by the military regime. Federalism was not constitutionally extinguished, but a strongly centralized regime was installed in political, fiscal and administrative terms. The weakening of the Federation did not mean, however, that regional elites ceased to be important in legitimizing the military regime. There has always been a need to carry out negotiations and distribute resources to local bases, especially to the poorest states. Ten years after the coup d'état, the military dictatorship began to lose economic momentum, international support and various social sectors began to organize against the regime. In this context, the elections for the Senate in 1974, with dynamics strongly linked to state politics, were the first moment in which the military lost control of the elections and the opposition began its process of rise. From then on, the regime gradually lost control of the political process.

The fight for democracy gained strength, particularly with the 1982 state elections, when opposition governors were elected. The balance of Brazilian history demonstrated a weak coupling between federalism and democracy. Moreover, for most of this historical trajectory, the quality of the Federative and democratic models was notably low. The process of redemocratization began to alter this narrative.

A new era for Democracy and Federalism: recent transformations and their challenges

The uniqueness of the recent Brazilian experience lies initially in the fact that the end of the dictatorship was strongly influenced by the marriage between federalism and democracy. It was forces that began winning local and, above all, state elections that led the opposition that overthrew the military regime. In 1982, opposition parties won the governments of the main Brazilian states. This created what Juan Linz (1983) called "dyarchy", as there were two types of government with power and legitimacy: the Federal Government chosen in an authoritarian manner and the governors elected democratically. This federative tension was fundamental to the end of authoritarianism, as opposition governors led political and social actors in a campaign to return to direct elections for the president. Despite having lost this legal battle, they managed to win the indirect elections in 1985, resulting in the former governor of the state (of Minas Gerais), Tancredo Neves, becoming the President (Abrucio, 1998).

A new federalism was enshrined in the 1988 Constitution, marking two important and non-contradictory trends. Firstly, there was the strengthening of the autonomy of states and municipalities, alongside the decentralization of resources and public policies. Secondly, there was the maintenance of the Federal Government as a fundamental pillar of the Federation, tasked with combating regional inequalities and coordinating intergovernmental relations linked to the policies of the Social Welfare State. Although significant power still resides with the Union in Brazilian federalism – especially at the normative, financial and bureaucratic levels – there has been a democratization of relations among the three federative entities and a strengthening of the federative safeguards of the States and, to a lesser extent, municipal governments. The contemporary Brazilian federalism exhibits five main characteristics. Firstly, it involves the creation of a triadic Federation, wherein municipalities are recognized as federative entities. Secondly, it entails the adoption of various fiscal and financial mechanisms aimed at reducing regional inequalities. Thirdly, it encompasses the expansion of the welfare state through robust decentralization coupled with federative coordination, leveraging the model of National Public Policy Systems. Fourthly, it involves the establishment of federative safeguards, promoting a more intergovernmental and less centralized governance model. Finally, as a fifth point, it encompasses the presence of incentives for federal competition and fragmentation, which impede effective governmental performance and the synergy between federalism and democracy.

Brazil has adopted a model of triadic federalism, in which municipalities became federative entities, something perhaps only similar to the South African case. Even so, the degree of political, tax and administrative autonomy of local power in Brazil, as well as the fact that the Federal Constitution prohibits the extinction or merger of municipalities (article 60), make the Brazilian experience even more peculiar. Formal local autonomy is strong, but there is a paradox here: the strong decentralization of competences and public services was carried out in a very unequal country, where most local governments have low state capacities (Grin, Demarco, & Abrucio, 2021). The main constitutive heterogeneity of the Brazilian Federation is territorial inequality (Arretche, 2012; Arretche, Schlegel, & Ferrari, 2015), clearly interconnected with the social inequality that marks Brazil.

Two characteristics of recent federalism act on this issue: the adoption of various financial instruments for federal redistribution of resources and the impressive increase in welfare policies, with federal coordination and subnational implementation. Regarding the first point, it is necessary to emphasize that Brazil has constitutionalized transfers to states and municipalities, with a high degree of formalization and with political or intergovernmental control mechanisms. About the expansion of social policies, the main characteristic is the creation of National Public Policy Systems. They are responsible for dividing government tasks and favoring federative interdependence between levels of government, especially through intergovernmental councils and instruments for inducing national standards of public policies (Bichir, Simoni Jr., & Pereira, 2020; Abrucio, Segatto, & Silva, 2023). The most successful case of these National Systems is in the sector of Health with the SUS (*Sistema Único de Saúde*), but there are good experiences in Social Assistance, Water Resources and, to a lesser extent, in educational policy.

The expansion of the Welfare State and the creation of national systems of federative coordination of public policies had the greatest result, in short, the strengthening of instruments to combat inequality, at the same time that they are more inserted in a democratic process of participation and guarantee of rights of federative entities. There was also an increase in federal safeguards (Schnabel, 2020) for states and municipalities, a central theme for analyzing the coupling between federalism and democracy. There are several mechanisms that have guaranteed such federative rights: intergovernmental public policy councils, the possibility of appeal to the Federal Supreme Court (STF), federative advocacy with political representatives in the National Congress and forms of horizontal cooperation between states and municipalities. The power of the Federal Government in Brazil is still very great, but federative checks and balances are increasingly powerful.

Obviously, there are still several problems in Brazilian federalism, due to the power and administrative asymmetry between the federative entities, the great territorial inequality and because Brazil has a still new experience of democratic federalism. Many public policies are poorly articulated in intergovernmental terms, such as environmental and public safety issues. There is also a long way to go to improve local state capabilities. Finally, there are characteristics of the political system that favor the fragmentation of resources and local clientelism, negatively affecting both democracy and federalism. Despite the problems and challenges, two issues highlight the progress made in recent years.

First, there was an expansion of the forms of coupling between federalism and democracy in Brazil. In summary, it is possible to list five aspects that generated positive combinations between the federative model and the democratic regime after the 1988 Constitution: 1) A more consociational democratic regime was established, expanding the checks and balances of the political system, with federalism being a central piece of this model. 2) State and municipal governments have become more autonomous, allowing for greater local accountability. Because of this, many local governments have built innovations in public policy and public service delivery that have increased voters' ability to choose from a more diverse range of options. Furthermore, this process facilitates dialogue and the dissemination of innovative models between federative entities. 3) The mechanisms of citizen participation and co-production of public services have expanded, especially at the subnational level, being yet another reflection of the greater connection between federalism and democracy. 4) Public policies organized by National Systems created federative forums in which subnational governments and other social actors negotiate and deliberate together. This model is one of the most successful examples of multilevel democratic governance in the Brazilian State. 5) Finally, although the issue of ethnic or linguistic diversity does not have the centrality in the Brazilian federation that it has in Belgium or India, there have been important advances in indigenous policy, largely due to the mechanisms that connect greater democratization (guarantee of rights) with much more effective federative policies than in the past – a proxy for this is that there were around 200 thousand indigenous people at the end of the military regime (1980s) and in 2023 Brazil had 1 million and 700 thousand indigenous people.

A second event reinforces the advances in the Brazilian case. The biggest test that the marriage between federalism and democracy has recently undergone was the Bolsonaro Government. Its objective was to weaken democracy and institute an autocratic project, and federalism was an obstacle to the Bolsonarist governance model (Abrucio et al., 2020). This political vision resulted in a huge conflict between the Federal Government and subnational governments, especially state governments, during this period of government (2019-2022). An uncoordinated and confrontational federalism was established, the culmination of which was the management of the COVID-19 pandemic. With his denialist and polarizing leadership, President Bolsonaro fought with governors and tried to boycott the participatory federative model of the Health System (SUS). Undeniably, Bolsonarism left negative marks, with around 700 thousand deaths, but the reaction of state governments, with the support of the Supreme Court (STF), the National Congress and the epistemic community that manages the Health System, avoided the worst. Federative autonomy was largely protected, municipalities, states and regions sought horizontal consortium solutions, and, consequently, Bolsonaro was unable to end the marriage between federalism and democracy (Abrucio, Grin, & Segatto, 2021).

Conclusion

The discussion of the Brazilian case clearly shows how federalism and democracy do not have a necessary link. Most of Brazilian history was one of absence or dissociation between the two. But, at the same time, the chapter revealed how the connection between the democratic regime and the federative model can be extremely positive. Brazil's recent experience is a very interesting case because it has produced many innovations and political and social advances by coupling the Federation with democratic institutions and processes in different ways. To explain the uniqueness of the Brazilian case, it is necessary to mobilize comparative institutional categories linked to federalism and democracy, but this path is not sufficient.

Three other elements are important to avoid an evolutionary and homogenizing view of Federations. The first is to understand what territorial heterogeneities constitute each case. In Brazil, the issue of territorial inequality is essential, as in other federations, such as Mexico and India, and with much greater weight than in federalisms of Anglo-Saxon origin or even Germany. There are other important diversities in Brazil, but the big question is how to find paths to democratic federalism, which guarantee autonomy and federative safeguards, with the reduction of territorially organized economic, social and political asymmetries. A second explanatory element that must be incorporated into comparative analyzes is to connect the study of institutions with political processes, in a line closer to historical neo-institutionalism. The greatest recent coupling between federalism and democracy was initially due to the way in which redemocratization occurred.

Furthermore, the theme of inequality, including territorial inequality, has been the great *leitmotif* of Brazilian politics in recent decades. This generated strong pressure for the expansion of the Welfare State, and this was only possible through governance that combined decentralization and federative coordination. This model generated the need, in different ways, to combine self-rule with shared rule. Evidently, political processes in Brazil have not always favored the coupling between federalism and democracy. Recently, President Bolsonaro's leadership produced lack of coordination and federative confrontation. For this reason, it is always necessary to analyze how the public agenda and the actions of the main political actors relate to the institutional model.

For example, the environmental issue is gaining a lot of strength in the Brazilian case, including due to international pressure. The Amazon Region has a series of peculiarities and difficulties in terms of territorial governance. This issue is already affecting the way in which federalism and Brazilian democracy work together to face this enormous challenge. Finally, instead of categorizing federalism into dual categories concerning its relationship with democracy, a more nuanced approach is proposed by Sonnicksen (2018; 2024): adopting a scale of forms of coupling. When analyzing the Brazilian case, it become apparent that this scale of coupling varies over time and may exhibit different positions within a single historical moment. A new analytical approach would be to understand the various degrees of coupling and decoupling that can exist between federalism and democracy in different countries, as well as the factors explaining this spectrum. This approach is believed to be the most effective in avoiding an evolutionist and even colonialist approach when making comparisons between Federations.

References

Abrucio, F. L. (1998). *Os barões da federação: Os governadores e a redemocratização brasileira*. São Paulo: Editora Hucitec.

Abrucio, F. L. et al. (2020). Combating COVID-19 under Bolsonaro's federalism: A case of intergovernmental incoordination. *Revista de Administração Pública*, 54, 663-677.

Abrucio, F. L., Segatto, C. I., & Silva, A. N. (2023). Sistemas nacionales de política social en Brasil y salvaguardas federales. In J. Mendoza Ruiz, & E. J. Grin (Orgs.), *Las salvaguardas federales en Argentina, Brasil y México: Relaciones, límites y contrapesos* (Vol. 1, pp. 283-316). Córdoba: Editorial Universidad Nacional de Córdoba.

Abrucio, F. L., Grin, E., & Segatto, C. I. (2021). Brazilian federalism in the pandemic. In B. G. Peters, E. J. Grin, & F. L. Abrucio (Orgs.), *American federal systems and COVID-19: Responses to a complex intergovernmental problem* (Vol. 1, pp. 63-88). Bingley: Emerald Publishing.

Arretche, M. (2012). *Democracia, federalismo e centralização no Brasil*. Rio de Janeiro: Editora FGV.

Arretche, M., Schlegel, R., & Ferrari, D. (2015). Preferences regarding the vertical distribution of authority in Brazil: On measurement and determinants. *Publius: The Journal of Federalism*, 46, 33-102.

Benz, A., & Broschek, J. (2013). *Federal dynamics: Continuity, change, and the varieties of federalism*. Oxford: Oxford University Press.

Broschek, J., Bettina, P., & Toubou, S. (2017). Territorial politics and institutional change: A comparative-historical analysis. *Publius: The Journal of Federalism*, 48(1), 1-25.

Burgess, M. (1993). Federalism and federation: A reappraisal. In M. Burgess, & A. Gagnon (Orgs.), *Comparative federalism and federation*. London: Harvester/Wheatsheaf.

Bichir, R., Júnior, S. S., & Pereira, G. (2020). Sistemas nacionais de políticas públicas e seus efeitos na implementação: O caso do Sistema Único de Assistência Social (Suas). *Revista Brasileira de Ciências Sociais*, 35(102), 1-23.

Dahl, R. (2001). *How Democratic is the American Constitution*. New Heaven: Yale University.

Dahl, R. (1986). Federalism and democratic process. In *Democracy, identity and equality* (pp. 114-126). Oslo: Norwegian University Press.

Elazar, D. J. (1987). *Exploring federalism*. Tuscaloosa: University of Alabama Press.

Grin, E. J., Demarco, D. J., & Abrucio, F. L. (Eds.). (2021). *Capacidades estatais municipais: O universo desconhecido no federalismo brasileiro*. Porto Alegre: Ed. CEGOV UFRGS.

Hagopian, F. (1996). *Traditional politics and regime change in Brazil*. Cambridge: Cambridge University Press.

Keyssar, Alexander (2020). *Why Do We Still Have the Electoral College?* Cambridge: Harvard University.

Linz, J. (1983). *The transition from the authoritarian regime to democracy in Spain: Some thoughts for Brazilians*. New Haven: Yale University.

Peters, B. G., Grin, E., & Abrucio, F. L. (2021). *American federal systems and COVID-19: Responses to a complex intergovernmental problem*. Bingley: Emerald Publishing.

Sallum Júnior, B. (1996). *Labirinto: Dos generais à Nova República*. São Paulo: Hucitec.

Samuels, D., & Abrucio, F. L. (2000). Federalism and democratic transitions: The new politics of the governors of Brazil. *Publius: The Journal of Federalism, 30*(2), 43-61.

Scharpf, F. W. (1988). The joint-decision trap: Lessons from German federalism and European integration. *Public Administration, 66*, 239-278.

Schnabel, J. (2020). *Managing interdependencies in federal systems: Intergovernmental councils and the making of public policy*. Cham: Palgrave Macmillan.

Sonnicksen, J. (2018). Federalism and democracy: A tense relationship. In J. Tudela, M. Kölling, & F. Reviriego (Eds.), *Calidad democrática y organización territorial* (pp. 31-52). Madrid: Marcial Pons.

Sonnicksen, J. (2024). *Federalism and democracy: Connections and challenges*. São Paulo: Mimeo.

Stepan, A. (1999). Para uma nova análise comparativa do federalismo e da democracia: Federações que restringem ou ampliam o poder do Demos. *Dados – Revista de Ciências Sociais, 42*(2), 197-251.

7

LOCAL GOVERNMENTS AS LABORATORIES OF DEMOCRATIC INNOVATIONS? THE ROLE OF NATIONAL COORDINATION AND INTERGOVERNMENTAL RELATIONS IN BRAZIL

Catarina Ianni Segatto

Introduction

There is a very well-known argument in the scholarship about federalism regarding the potential of federal systems to boost local innovations. Some scholars argue that subnational autonomy fosters local innovations, and enhances democracy and accountability, referring to local governments as the "laboratories" of democratic innovations (Osborne, 1988). Subnational autonomy also allows the diffusion of innovations among jurisdictions (Shipan & Volden, 2008). The Brazilian case reinforces these arguments, as civil society and local governments played a key role in constructing important participatory innovative policies and arenas. Decentralization allowed the development of democratic innovations by subnational governments, such as Participatory Budgeting, which was created in the municipality of Porto Alegre in 1989 (De Oliveira, 2017).

Brazil's case also shows the limitations of these ideas, as national coordination was crucial for ensuring the institutionalization of social participation across the country, as argued in the scholarship on federalism (Obinger, Leibfried, & Castles, 2005). The return to democracy, particularly the approval of the 1988 Constitution, was critical for institutionalizing participatory innovative policies and arenas at all three levels – federal government, states, and municipalities. The 1988 Constitution also established a federal model that combines decentralization and centralization, wherein the federal government holds significant decision-making powers, enabling the strengthening of national coordination in different policies over time (Arretche, 2012). This was essential to increase subnational governments' state capacities, including participatory policy councils and committees (Arretche et al., 2012; Grin, 2016; Grin & Abrucio, 2019; Lavalle, Rodrigues, & Guicheney, 2019; Lavalle, Guicheney, & Bezerra, 2023).

Seeking to discuss the intersections between federalism and democratic innovations, this chapter provides a brief contextualization of the Brazilian case and a systematization of crucial research questions that guide the debate about federalism and democratic innovations in Brazil. These questions include subnational variation, social participation de-institutionalization, and multilevel governance.

1. Brazil's path of democratic innovations

The 1988 Constitution universalized social policies and established a model that combines centralized and decentralized features. The federal government, states, and municipalities share powers in most policies. While the federal government plays an important role in setting national guidelines and funding subnational governments, it also serves as a primary decision-maker in certain policies. At the same time, states and municipalities are critical in-service provision.

The new Constitution also determined the institutionalization of social participation. An example of this includes the institutionalized policy councils in various sectors, including those outlined in "articles 194 (social security), 198 (healthcare), 204 (welfare), 206 (education) and 227 (child and adolescent)" (De Oliveira, 2017, p. 9). At the national level, the first such council was the National Health Council, which is responsible for making decisions about different aspects of health policy, setting national guidelines and funding, and overseeing and auditing the decisions and spending of the Ministry of Health. It comprises representatives of all three levels of government – federal, states, and municipal – as well as service providers, organizations representing users, and health professionals. Similar councils and committees were established in other public policies areas, though in some cases, there are significant differences in the profiles of the representatives and their powers.

It is important to note that, in certain public policies, the Brazilian case has combined policy councils and other participatory committees with intergovernmental arenas. Discussing subnational representation in participatory institutional bodies is crucial for understanding their role in decision-making, going beyond their representation in the second chamber and intergovernmental commissions. For example, the Intermanagers Commission plays a limited role in healthcare, involving only the three levels of government. It makes decisions concerning operational, financial, and administrative aspects of the public healthcare system, and formulates national, regional, and inter-municipal guidelines. While the National Health Council plays a more critical role in national decision-making, the representation of subnational governments has been restricted; they have only had two seats since the 1990s, despite the total number of seats increasing from 32 to 50 during that time (Segatto & Béland, 2021, p. 11).

At the local level, there are different types of social participation, such as Participatory Budgeting, public hearings, conferences, and policy councils. It is important to note that some experiences predated the return to democracy, including participatory institutional bodies (such as base ecclesial communities, workplace committees, political party groups, and community health committees) and conferences, which had been organized by the *sanitaristas*, a social movement that strongly influenced the health chapter of the 1988 Constitution (Bezerra, 2020).

The 1988 Constitution, by guaranteeing subnational autonomy, enabled subnational governments to develop innovative policies. For instance, the *Bolsa Escola* programme, initiated in two municipalities (Campinas and Brasília), which inspired the *Bolsa Família* program, and the community health workers, created in the state of Ceará and transformed in a national programme a few years later (Paulics, 2004; Tendler, 1998). Moreover, the Participatory Budgeting, created by the Workers' Party in Porto Alegre in 1989, seeking to ensure social participation in the decisions and deliberations of policies, was diffused by other municipalities in which the Workers' Party won during the 1990s. However, by 2001, other political parties had adopted almost half of the Participatory Budgeting experiences (Wampler, 2008).

The diffusion of the Participatory Budgeting and policy councils was not solely driven by partisanship but also by networks, politicians, and non-government organizations that promoted specific ideas related to the importance of social participation for democracy and accountability, as well as public policies aimed at meeting citizens' needs. These ideas gained traction during the transition to democracy, as there was an expectation that decentralization would enhance democracy. Consequently, democratic innovations were associated with the belief that proximity to the people leads to more democratic decisions and better addressing of local needs and issues, although this notion was challenged in subsequent decades (Arretche, 1996).

During the 1990s and 2000s, the strengthening of national coordination institutionalized participatory bodies. Various changes included the establishment of minimum national standards, mechanisms for redistributing resources, project grants (through federal programs linked to voluntary transfers), information and evaluation systems, and intergovernmental arenas, resulting in the creation of "national public policy systems" (Bichir, Simoni Jr, & Pereira, 2020; Franzese & Abrucio, 2013).

These changes facilitated the dissemination of public policies across states and municipalities, with implications for the development of subnational state capacities, including financial, administrative, and social participation dimensions, reducing regional inequalities regarding access to public policies in the country (Arretche et al., 2012; Bichir, Simoni Jr, & Pereira, 2020; Grin, 2016; Grin & Abrucio, 2019; Lavalle, Rodrigues, & Guicheney, 2019; Lavalle, Guicheney, & Bezerra, 2023). Regarding social participation capacities at the subnational level, policy councils were spread out across the country, particularly at the municipal level, and were associated with different public policies. In 2014, for instance, there were 62,562 policy councils in Brazilian municipalities (De Porto, 2017). These policy councils comprise representatives from governments and civil society (often representatives of organized interest groups), responsible for decision-making and the oversight and monitoring of public policies.

2. Recent debates

Subnational variation. An important topic that has been greatly discussed in Brazil refers to the variation among participatory institutional bodies. These bodies are associated with different public policies, vary in the groups of societal actors that are represented (dividing differently the number of seats between governmental and societal actors), and influence different decision-making, as they can vary in their powers (deliberative, consultative, monitoring, and auditing), and the dynamics of its functioning (Almeida et al., 2015).

Recent studies have focused on understanding the factors that explain similarities and differences in the characteristics and activities of participatory institutional bodies at the local level. These studies highlight that the institutionalization of policy councils varied among public policies and Brazilian states. Lavalle, Guicheney, & Bezerra, (2023) show that territorial expansion and operation of municipal councils in environmental and heritage policy fields resulted from policy legacies, economic and sociodemographic contexts, state capacities, and associative density. However, the primary explanatory factors for their territorial expansion and operation are the state-level regulatory frameworks, which consist of sets of state norms in each policy area. In contexts with low national standardization, a state-level variation, influenced by the state governments' coordinative role, affects councils' functioning at the municipal level.

Future studies could explore the differences in the institutionalization of social participation across the country, particularly the role of state governments in this process. If it is a consensus that national coordination was key to the institutionalization of policy councils in states and municipalities, little is known about the effects of state governments' coordination in this process.

Social participation de-institutionalization. Recent changes have altered this path of institutionalization of social participation. In 2018, Jair Bolsonaro won the election with a discourse that combined neoliberal proposals with a right-wing populist rhetoric centered on conservative moral values, reinforcing traditional family notions, denying gender issues, emphasizing the opposition between the elite and "corrupt" others and the Brazilian people, and rejecting diversity and recognition. Based on this discourse, since the beginning of his government, nongovernmental organizations (NGOs), particularly those focused on rights and grassroots activism, have been closely monitored and targeted. They have lost funding, and their participation in policy formulation has been restricted (Segatto, Alves, & Pineda, 2023).

Within this context, numerous participatory institutional bodies have been abolished, especially through the approval of Decree 9,759/2019. Bezerra et al. (2023), analyzing the changes that affected councils and committees, show that 96 were de-institutionalized. The environment policy sector was the most affected, with 31% of committees or councils dissolved, while human rights experienced the highest rate of (45% of them modified). The authors also highlight that participatory institutional bodies in social policies were less affected as they were more deeply institutionalized.

Bezerra et al. (2023) highlight that, even in more institutionalized policy fields, there has been a decrease in social participation at the national level during the last four years. Some councils and committees kept functioning as laws determined them and could not be extinguished by a Presidential decree. Still, they suffered changes in their composition, including a reduction in the number of representatives from civil society or alterations to their activities, dynamics and representation (Segatto, Alves, & Pineda, 2023).

Future studies could explore the differences among policy fields, as some seem more resilient than others. Bezerra, Almeida, Lavalle and Dowbor (2024) showed, there were significant differences among policy fields, which is explained by the degree of institutionalization of participatory institutional bodies. In some policy fields, policy councils were more institutionalized, which impedes their extinction. Understanding the factors that explain this institutionalization and resilience over time would be fundamental, including analysis about the role of civil society and policy communities at institutionalizing these arenas, and the role of "national public policy systems" in the institutionalization processes.

Multilevel governance. Another important agenda is related to the role of actors, agency, and interactions in participatory institutional bodies through a multilevel perspective. In some public policies, specific actors were fundamental in promoting democratic innovations within political parties, civil society organizations, or social movements, which circulated between levels of government, influencing both the institutionalization of social participation and policy-making within them (Bezerra, 2020; Dowbor, 2012; Gibson, 2016; Harris, 2017).

However, little is known about this topic in different public policies, including how members of civil society organizations with seats in national participatory institutional bodies are linked or participate in networks and communities with members of civil society organizations with seats in subnational participatory institutional bodies. Moreover, it would be interesting to better grasp if they circulate among participatory institutional bodies, particularly during changes such as Bolsonaro's government. If changes at the national level influenced societal actors' strategies, and if and how the federal context allowed them to act on participatory institutional bodies at the subnational level, influencing policy-making.

3. Final remarks

The Brazilian experience demonstrates that subnational autonomy played a crucial role in enabling states and municipalities to foster democratic innovations. This was achieved by democratizing the policymaking process through the institutionalization of social participation, the involvement of new social actors in decision-making, and the development of public policies to address local challenges. Nevertheless, national coordination was essential to ensure the dissemination and institutionalization of participatory institutional bodies across the country. This was part of a broader effort to enhance subnational state capacities and mitigate regional inequalities.

To further explore this discourse, recent studies on federalism and democratic innovations in Brazil call attention to new research questions: subnational variation of the institutionalization of social participation among regions and the role of state governments' coordination in institutionalizing social participation; social participation de-institutionalization, particularly the differences among public policy fields in this process; and analysis of social participation through a multilevel governance perspective by understanding the role of actors, agency, and interactions within federal contexts and dynamics.

It is important to note that Lula's government, in its first year (2023), rebuilt participatory institutional bodies at the national level, dismantled by Bolsonaro's government, and proposed a new agenda of expanding and strengthening participatory institutional bodies and mechanisms, including mechanisms of e-participation. It is fundamental that future studies conduct a historical analysis of the changes in democratic innovations at both the national and subnational levels over time, particularly the effects of the variations in national coordination in subnational participatory institutional bodies and mechanisms."

References

Almeida, C., Cayres, D. C., & Tatagiba, L. (2015). Balanço dos estudos sobre os conselhos de políticas públicas na última década. *Lua Nova: Revista de Cultura e Política*, 255-294.

Arretche, M. (1996). Mitos da descentralização: mais democracia e eficiência nas políticas públicas. *Revista Brasileira de Ciências Sociais*, 11(31), 44-66.

Arretche, M. (2012). *Democracia, federalismo e centralização no Brasil*. Rio de Janeiro: FGV.

Arretche, M. et al. (2012). *Capacidades administrativas dos municípios brasileiros para a política habitacional*. São Paulo/Brasília: CEM/CEBRAP, Secretaria Nacional de Habitação/Ministério das Cidades.

Bezerra, C. D. P. (2020). *Ideologia e governabilidade: as políticas participativas nos governos do PT* [Doctoral dissertation, Universidade de São Paulo].

Bezerra, C.; Almeida, D. R.; Lavalle, A. G. and Dowbor, M. (2024). Desinstitucionalização e resiliência dos conselhos no governo Bolsonaro. *Dados*, 67 (4): 1-49.

Bichir, R., Simoni Junior, S., & Pereira, G. (2020). Sistemas nacionais de políticas públicas e seus efeitos na implementação o caso do Sistema Único de Assistência Social (SUAS). *Revista Brasileira de Ciências Sociais, 35*.

De Oliveira, O. P. (2017). *International policy diffusion and participatory budgeting: ambassadors of participation, international institutions and transnational networks.* London: Springer.

De Oliveira, O. P. (2017). Promovendo conexões transnacionais: As redes e a difusão do Orçamento Participativo. *Revista Brasileira de Políticas Públicas e Internacionais*, 2 (1): 4-35.

Dowbor, M. W. D. (2012). *A arte da institucionalização: estratégias de mobilização dos sanitaristas (1974-2006)* [Doctoral dissertation, Universidade de São Paulo].

Franzese, C., & Abrucio, F. L. (2013). Efeitos recíprocos entre federalismo e políticas públicas no Brasil: os casos dos sistemas de saúde, de assistência social e de educação. In: G. Hochman and C. A. Faria (Eds.). *Federalismo e políticas públicas no Brasil* (pp. 361-386). Rio de Janeiro: Editora Fiocruz.

Gibson, C. L. (2016). Sanitaristas, Petistas, and the Post-Neoliberal Public Health State in Porto Alegre. *Latin American Perspectives, 43*(2), 153-171.

Grin, E. (2016). *Rotas federativas para a promoção de capacidades estatais municipais: uma análise da experiência brasileira* [Doctoral dissertation, Fundação Getulio Vargas].

Grin, E., & Abrucio, F. L. (2019). Las capacidades estatales de los municipios brasileños en un contexto de descentralización de políticas. *Revista del CLAD Reforma y Democracia, 70*, 93-126.

Harris, J. (2017). "Professional movements" and the expansion of access to healthcare in the industrializing world. *Sociology of Development, 3*(3), 252-272.

Lavalle, A. G., Guicheney, H., & Bezerra, C. (2023). O papel dos estados na normatização dos conselhos municipais de políticas públicas. In Palotti, P., Licio, E. C., Sandra, G., Catarina Ianni, S., & André Luis Nogueira Da, S. (Eds.), *E os Estados? Federalismo, relações intergovernamentais e políticas públicas no Brasil contemporâneo* (pp. 237-264). Rio de Janeiro: Ipea.Lavalle, A. G., Rodrigues, M., & Guicheney, H. (2019). Agência local e indução federal: A operação da política municipal de habitação em Recife e Curitiba. *Revista de Sociologia e Política, 27*(71), 1-27.

Obinger, H.; Leibfried, S.; Castles, F. G. (Eds.). (2005). *Federalism and the welfare state: New World and European experiences.* Cambridge: Cambridge University, 2005.

Osborne, D. (1988). *Laboratories of democracy.* Harvard: Harvard Business School Press.

Paulics, V. (2004). Disseminação de experiências de gestão pública: o caso do Programa de Renda Mínima no Brasil (1991-1997). *Cadernos Gestão Pública e Cidadania, 9*(34).

Segatto, C. I., & Béland, D. (2021). Federalism and decision making in health care: the influence of subnational governments in Brazil. *Policy Studies, 42*(3), 308-326.

Segatto, C. I., Alves, M. A., & Pineda, A. (2023). Uncivil society and social policies in Brazil: The backlash in the gender, sexual, and reproductive rights and ethnic and racial relations fields. *Public Administration and Development, 43*(1), 60-69.

Shipan, C. R. & Volden, C. (2008). The mechanisms of policy diffusion. *American Journal of Political Science, 4*(52), 840-857.

Tendler, J. (1998). *Bom Governo nos Trópicos: Uma visão crítica.* Revan: ENAP.

Wampler, B. (2008). When does participatory democracy deepen the quality of democracy? Lessons from Brazil. *Comparative politics, 41*(1), 61-81.

FEDERALISM AND TERRITORIAL RESPONSES TO DIVERSITY IN AFRICA AND THEIR IMPLICATIONS

Zemelak Ayitenew Ayele

Introduction

Africa has over 3000 distinct ethnic communities and over 2100 linguistic communities. There are however only 54 countries on the continent. This means almost every African state has an ethnically, linguistically, and religiously diverse population. On average, every African country has 55 ethnic communities. Indeed, the diversity is different from one country to the other. Countries, such as Nigeria, have hundreds of ethnic and linguistic communities while countries such as Somalia have ethnically and religiously homogenous population. Even the Somalis are divided along clan lines. Besides, ethnic communities are divided along international boundaries due to the randomly drawn colonial boundaries which did not take into account the settlement patterns of communities. The Somalis are found in four African countries – Somalia, Ethiopia, Kenya, and Djibouti. The Wolof ethnic community is found in Senegal, Gambia, and Mauritania and the Fulani are found in close to 20 countries including Nigeria, Cameroon, Senegal, and Mali while the Igbo are found in Nigeria, Cameroon, Equatorial Guinea, and Gabon. The people have to live with the boundaries created by colonial powers due to the principle of *uti possidetis juris* (UPJ) – a principle of international law that requires states emerging from colonial rule to retain the colonial boundaries (Mnyongani, 2008).

At independence, almost all African states found that it was imperative to implement a project of nation-building if they were to exist as functioning states (Bandyopadhyay & Green, 2013). Each state sought to create a nation-state out of the various ethnic communities that were found within its boundaries. To this effect, they introduced centralised system since the alternative would presumably have provided a favourable context for inter-ethnic rivalry. Many of the sub-Saharan African states introduced a single-party system, among others, in the name of nation-building. Only a handful of African countries implemented a federal system that aimed at territorially responding to the ethnic diversity of the people. Even those quickly abandoned their federal projects and implemented centralised system (Erk, 2023). Despite the rhetoric of nation-building and establishing a nation-state, politics in Africa was usually based on ethnicity. One would come to power or would be removed from power because of his or her ethnic affiliation. Democracy was in a short supply and military *coups* were very frequent in Africa, with over 240 successful and attempted coups, so that Africa has the highest number of coups in the world (Duzor & Williamson, 2023). This was the context in Africa between the 1960s and 1990s.

In the 1990s, following the fall of the Berlin Wall, which symbolized the end of communism, there was a push for democratization both internally and externally and, as part of that push for democratization, there was also a demand for some form of a devolved system (Gedlu, 1997). Thus, beginning from the early 1990s, several African countries adopted some kind of federal arrangement or devolved system. Among the African states that adopted devolved/federal system are South Africa, Ethiopia, Nigeria, Sudan, Congo, Kenya, South Sudan, Somalia and Zimbabwe.

In terms of territorially dealing with diversity, the African countries adopted one of the two approaches. The first is to demarcate internal boundaries exclusively based on ethnic criteria. The other was an approach that took ethnicity and geographic, economic, administrative, and other factors. The paper explains how the two important federal or quasi-federal countries in Africa, Kenya and Nigeria, tried the first approach at independence, but immediately abandoned it since each state faced different challenges as a result of the federal design. Ethiopia, the other important federal country in Africa, adopted the same approach decades after Nigeria and Kenya abandoned this approach. Ethiopia faces similar challenges to those faced by Nigeria and Kenya. However, it is unclear whether and how it will revise its federal design. The paper will describe the territorial design and the federal experiences of the three countries and ends with concluding remarks.

Kenya

Kenya has over 40 ethnic communities and none of them is in majority at the national level even if the Kikuyu, Luhya, Luo, Kalenjin, and the like are among the major ethnic communities of the country. There are also smaller communities such as the Massai, Meru, and Kisii (Statistica, 2019). The debate on how to territorially respond to the ethnic diversity of the country preceded the country's independence in 1963 (Anderson, 2005). Two political parties took part in the negotiation towards independence from the British colonial administration: the Kenyan Africa National Union (KANU) and the Kenyan Africa Democratic Union (KADU) (Anderson, 2005). The first political party was made up of representatives of the major ethnic communities, such as Kikuyu, Luo, Kamba, Meru, and Embu. Its leaders included Jamo Kenyatta, the first president of Kenya. Members of the KANU sought to gain independence immediately. They also wanted to establish a unitary and centralized system in Kenya. On the other hand, afraid of being dominated by the larger ethnic communities once Kenya became independent, members of the KADU, representing smaller ethnic communities, such as the Kalenjin, Maasai, Turkana, and Samburu where were the view that Kenya's independence should not be rushed. They were also insistent that an independent Kenya should have a federal system, with ethnically organized sub-national territorial units. The colonial administration agreed with KANU and the independence constitution entrenched a federal system which was locally known as majimbo, a Swahili word that means region. Eight provinces or regions were created whose 'boundaries were similar to the provincial boundaries of the colonial PA (that is, drawn along ethnic lines), albeit with minor alterations (Bosire, 2013).

As can be seen in the map below, the provinces were relatively large and the major ethnic communities had their homeland provinces.

Figure 1. The map of Kenya at independence with ethnically demarcated provincial boundaries

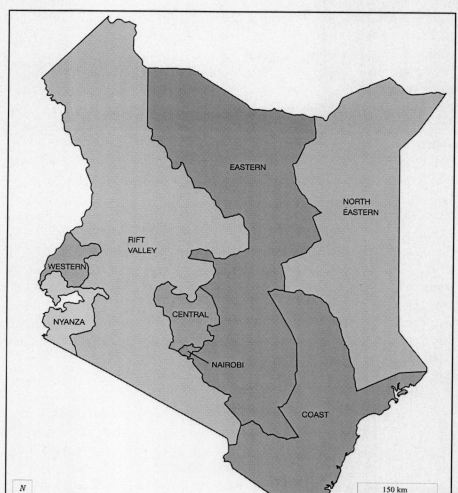

Source: https://www.un.int/kenya/kenya/general-information-about-kenya

As mentioned KADU, the political party of the small ethnic communities, initially succeeded in having an ethnic federal system entrenched in the 1963 constitution. It was not however able to ensure the proper implementation of the independence constitution since it lost to KANU in the first national election (Bosire, 2013). KANU soon began introducing various measures that led to the undoing of the regions until majimbo was abolished altogether in 1968. As far as KANU was concerned, the regions were too expensive to maintain, and that majimbo led to inter-ethnic competition which undermined the nation-building project. It also allegedly provided a favorable context for ethnic-based competition and demand for land (Boon, 2012). Some secessionist movements emerged in northern Kenya and coastal areas immediately after Kenya gained its independence (Thomas & Falola, 2020). Under the pretext of nation-building, KANU entrenched a centralized system and Jammo Kenyatta's rule (Kwatemba, 2008). Kenya became even more centralized under Daniel Arap Moi, the country's second president, who officially introduced a one-party system where only KANU has the right to exist (Kadima & Owuor, 2014). Other opposition parties were banned.

The centralized system was however unpopular since it led to the political marginalization of different communities and unequal development in the country. Beginning in the early 1900s, different political and civic organizations began advocating for an inclusive multiparty democracy and the end of Arap Moi's authoritarian system. As part of the push for opening up the political space, there was a demand for a decentralized system. The single-party system came to an end in 1992 when the constitution was amended to remove the clause entrenching a single-party system. The issue of whether and how to introduce decentralized system was continuously debated for an additional two decades until it was settled with the adoption of the 2010 constitution. At the heart of the controversy was whether to re-introduce the majimbo system, which provided a homeland for the major ethnic communities, or another version of decentralized system (Bosire, 2013). The final result of the constitution reform process of a devolved system that skewed the former ethnic-based provinces as units of devolution. Instead, 47 counties, each of which has an ethnic majority but is much smaller than the provinces of the majimbo era were created.

Figure 2. Kenya's political map

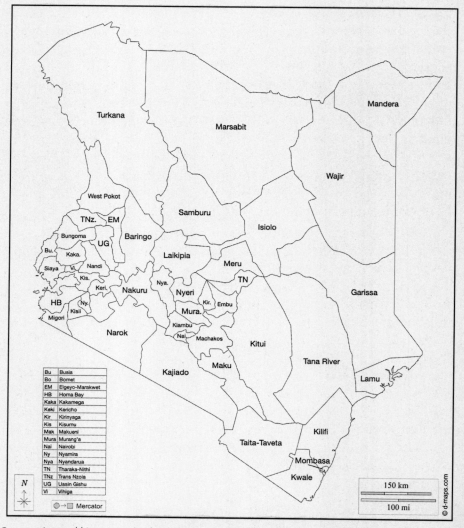

Source: https://d-maps.com/carte.php?num_car=239&lang=pt

As can be seen in Table 1 below, the devolved system led to the division of the major ethnic communities into different counties. Now the largest ethnic communities, such as the Kikuyu and the Luo are divided into up to 10 counties. The relatively smaller communities, such as the Kissi, also have their counties. Every county, save for Nairobi, has an ethnic community that is in the majority. The devolved system thus responds to the self-administration or the self-rule demand of most of the ethnic communities of the country without however giving a single homeland for an ethnic community. None of the ethnic communities is now enclosed in a single province as was the case in the 1960s (Nyabira & Ayele, 2016).

Table 1. Counties where various ethnic communities form the majority

Ethnic communities	Counties
Kalenjin	Uasin Gishu, Kericho, Bomet, 'Nandi', Baringo
Kikuyu	Kiambu, Muranga, Nyandarua, Nyeri, Kirinyaga, Nakuru, Laikipia
Luo	Siaya, Kisumu, Migori, Homa-Bay
Luhya	Kakamega, Vihiga, Bungoma, Busia, Trans-Nzoia
Kamba	Makueni, Machakos, Kitui
Kisii	Kisii, Nyamira
Meru	Meru, Tharaka-Nithi
Embu	Embu
Maasai	Samburu, Narok, Kajiado
Somali	Garissa, Wajir, Mandera
Turkana	Turkana
Borana	Marsabit, Isiolo
Waswahili, Durma, Giriama, Rabai, Boni, Digo,	Mombasa
Mijikenda	Kwale, Kilifi, Tana River, Lamu
Taita	Taita Taveta
Pokot	West Pokot
Marakwet	Elgeyo Marakwet
Mixed	Nairobi

Source: Nyabira & Ayele (2016)

What is the implication of this arrangement? Studies show that the devolved system has increased access to social services as most decentralized systems do. It has created a sense and a framework of inclusion for many hitherto marginalized ethnic communities without making ethnicity the sole factor of the subnational territorial organization of the country. It has also reduced the incidence of political violence in the country. This does not mean that devolution did away with ethnic politics in Kenya. Ethnicity is still very important in Kenyan politics. The presidency remains the most important political position and people contest for the position along ethnic lines. Ethnic alliances are formed before and during periods of presidential election. However, the creation of other political positions, such as county governorship, has reduced the intensity of the ethnic-based contestations for the presidency.

Nigeria

Nigeria is the oldest federation in Africa. Its journey towards a federal system began when it was still under the colonial rule of Britain (Afigbo, 1991). It started its federal arrangement using three extremely large regions as subnational units. As can be seen in figure 3, the three regions were the North, the South-West, and the South-East. Each of the three regions had an ethnic majority. In the North, the Hausa-Fulani, predominantly Muslim, constitute an ethnic majority. In the South-West, the Yoruba, have both Christian and Muslim faiths, and in the East, the predominantly Christian Igbo ethnic communities constitute the majority (Suberu, 2023). Indeed, over 300 ethnic communities are found in Nigeria, but the Hausa-Fulani, the Yoruba, and the Igbo are the major ethnic communities in the country. Thus, when the federal system of the country was established, the three regions that were demarcated along ethnic lines, and which were considered homelands of the three major ethnic communities, were used as subnational units (Yimenu, 2024).

Figure 3. Nigeria and the three regions

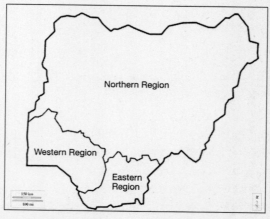

Source: https://joshksnigeriaproject.yolasite.com/

The Nigerian federal system was initially extremely unbalanced. The northern region was in territorial and population terms larger than the two southern regions combined (Veenendaal & Demarest, 2021). It represented about 70% of the total territorial area of Nigeria and over 50% of the country's population (Suberu, 2022). There was also an imbalance in terms of the distribution of economic resources and social services. The two southern regions, which were under direct British colonial rule, were in a better condition in this regard as compared to the northern region. These imbalances and the competition among the three regions (ethnic communities) undermined the federal system. The northern region in particular rivaled the federal government, which with its parliamentary form of government, was too weak to compete with the regions. Besides, the regions enjoyed significantly wide functional areas and political powers under the constitution. The three regions competed to dominate the center. All these factors undermined the functioning of the federal system. Nigeria became independent in 1960 with such a poorly functioning federal system in place (Veenendaal & Demarest, 2021). Among others, the malfunction of the federal system led to a military coup merely six years after the country gained its independence. From 1966 until 1999, Nigeria was basically under military rule with intermittent civilian rule. Those at the helm of the various military governments, centrist in their political mindset, introduced several reforms that led to the division of the three regions.

Nigeria now has 36 states which constitute the subnational units of the Nigerian federation. Almost each of the existing 36 states has an ethnic majority. However, none of the three major ethnic communities has a regional ethnic homeland any longer. This lessened the regional pressure on the center since there is no large region contending or competing with it. The states have become smaller and much weaker than before and the center has been relieved of regional pressure. The breaking up of the three regions has also reduced the threat of secession.

Figure 4. Nigeria and the 36 states

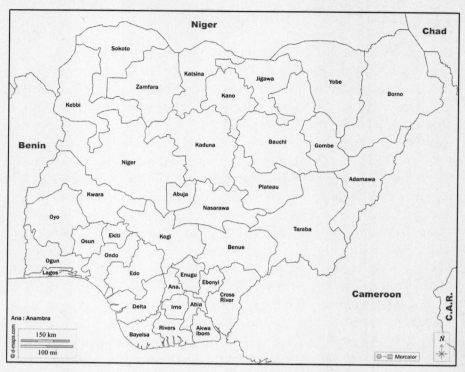

Source: https://d-maps.com/carte.php?num_car=4867

As Suberu (2022) argues, there is no secession group in Nigeria that poses a real threat to the territorial integrity of the country. The creation of numerous states that divide ethnic communities into several states has also created intra-ethnic community rivalry. Those who are from the same community but living in neighboring states now compete against each other for access to resources at the federal level. This does not however mean that regional identities no longer have political salience. Regional identities are still important. The unwritten rule for regionally rotating presidency is an indication of the significance of regional identities. Ethnicity and regional representation are also important considerations when it comes to the composition of civil administrative organs and the military. Nigeria has so-called the Federal Character Commission which is charged with checking that every ethnic community and region is fairly represented in every federal organ (Suberu, 2022). The re-organization of the subnational units had undoubtedly made the Nigerian federation a much more stable one than was the case in the 1960s.

Ethiopia

In the past, Ethiopia had projected itself as an Amharic-speaking and Orthodox Christian national state despite being a country of over 80 ethnic communities and diverse religions. It attempted to implement a nation-state-building project when it was an empire that ceased to exist after Haile Selassie I, the last emperor of the country was overthrown in 1974 by a military junta known as the Derg. The Derg also adopted the 'Ethiopia first' motto and suppressed demands for institutional reform aimed at managing the ethnic diversity of the country's population. This led to different conflicts and 17 years of civil war which ended in 1991 when the Ethiopian Peoples' Revolutionary Democratic Front (EPRDF) came to power having overthrown the Derg. EPRDF, with 24 other ethnically organized political organizations laid the foundation for the current ethnic federal system when it adopted the Transitional Period Charter in June 1991. The Charter recognized the right to self-determination of all ethnic communities including their right to unconditionally secede from the country.[4] The federal system was entrenched when the 1995 constitution was adopted.

As mentioned, the Ethiopian federal system is based on the recognition of the right to self-determination of ethnic communities which finds expression in that each ethnic community can enjoy territorial autonomy at the subnational level regardless of its population size and economic condition (Art 39(3), Constitution 1995). The territorial autonomy involves establishing subnational government that exercises certain legislative, executive and judicial powers. This is why the federation is often considered to be a federation of ethnic communities, not a federation of territories (Selassie, 2003). The constitution does not guarantee the territorial integrity of the country. Quite the contrary, it allows ethnic communities to secede from it and become an independent state. The constitution hence establishes a potentially breakable federal union.

---

[4] The right of ethnic communities to secede from the federation is unconditional in the sense an ethnic community does not need to justify why it should be allowed to secede. There are however certain procedural requirements that have to be followed in order to secede from the federation including the adoption with two-third majority of a resolution to secede by the council of the ethnic community, holding and referendum within three years which has to be supported by the majority of members of the relevant ethnic community, the transfer of power to the newly established state, and division of assets. See art 39(4) of the FDRE Constitution 1995.

The federal system allows ethnic communities to establish their state based on territorial settlement patterns (Art 47, Constitution 1995).[5] Thus, in principle, every ethnic community is entitled to a state of its own. Currently, the federation is made up of 12 states. The original members of the federation were nine in number. Five of the nine original states (Afar, Amhara, Oromia, Tigray, and Somali) are considered the homelands of the ethnic community whose name they bear. Oromia represents the largest and, with 35 percent of the Ethiopian population, the most populous state in the country followed by Amhara which, with 22 percent of the population, is the second most populous state. The Somali state is, next to Oromia, the second largest state even if, with just 6 percent of the Ethiopian population, is among the least populated states. These and the other mono-ethnic states including Tigray, Sidama, and Afar are likely to remain the same in terms of population and territorial size given the fact that they are considered as homeland of a single ethnic community.

Figure 5. Ethiopian federal map

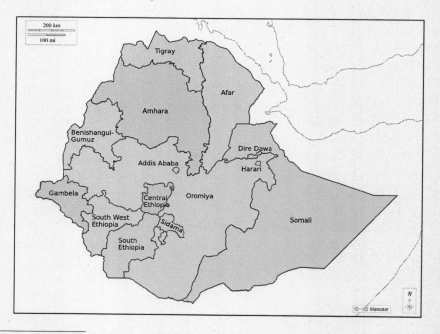

---

[5] The procedure for establishing a state is defined under Article 47(3) of the constitution which includes the adoption with two-third majority of a resolution to establish a state by the council of the ethnic community, holding and referendum within a year which has to be supported by the majority of members of the relevant ethnic community, the transfer of power to the newly established state, and division of assets.

Source: https://en.wikipedia.org/wiki/Regions_of_Ethiopia#/media/File:Regions_of_Ethiopia_EN.svg

The rest of the states are multi-ethnic states having no dominant ethnic community within them. Besides, the constitution contains a principle that every ethnic community, regardless of its population size its economic status, or whether or not it has the capacity to run a state, is entitled to a state of its own (Fessha & Ayele, 2021). It is based on this principle that the additional three states were created out of the former SNNP state which no longer exists. Thus, the smaller and multi-ethnic states are likely to get smaller as more and more ethnic communities secede from them while the large states, such as Oromia and Somali states, would remain the same. Moreover, an ethnic community cannot have more than one region. So large ethnic communities such as the Oromo are enclosed in a single state. Sub-ethnic historical identities do not find territorial expression in the current federal dispensation. This is what Yonatan Fessha calls 'the original sin' of this ethnic federal arrangement, which did not take into account subnational ethnic identity (Fessha, 2017). Hence the federal system had states with unbalanced territories and population from the very beginning making the federation unhealthy. This imbalance will only worsen and the federation will be even more unhealthy as new states are formed. The situation is exacerbated by the fact that the central government, which was in the past very strong because of the party in power, is now facing pressure from regional powers and it is becoming weak and facing both political and military challenges from the regions. A case in point is the military confrontation between the Tigray state and the federal government which the latter came close to losing.

It is important to note that the federal system has several positive sides. It has allowed those who were marginal communities, who were marginalized both in political and cultural terms, to be included in the political and cultural life of the country. It has also the effect of localizing conflicts because before it was a war between armed groups and the central government; now many smaller conflicts are not necessarily against the central government. In that regard, it has localized interethnic or other conflicts. However, it has the effect of making ethnicity the sole and the most important political factor. Politics in the country begins and ends with ethnicity (Fessha, 2010).

Conclusion

Kenya and Nigeria experimented with a federal system that sought to provide the major ethnic communities of the countries with a subnational homeland. They abandoned this federal design since it was too unbalanced and dysfunctional to sustain. Decades after the two countries redesigned their federal systems, Ethiopia adopted a federal system that is based on the same logic and design as the ones Kenya and Nigeria abandoned. It established a federal system that seeks to allow each of its ethnic communities to have a state of its own. Ethiopia is facing challenges similar to those that Kenya and Nigeria faced when they were implementing their federal systems which were exclusively based on ethnic criteria. One way for Ethiopia to deal with the challenges that the federal system brought about would be to renegotiate the constitution and redesign the federal arrangement. However, this is not likely because the elites of some of the major ethnic communities, such as the Oromos, the Tigray, and the Somalis, are in favor of the current arrangement. Thus, one cannot expect the political elites of the country to sit down and renegotiate the constitutional arrangement and devise another kind of federal arrangement. The other option would be, as was the case in Kenya and Nigeria, for the federal government to unilaterally redesign the federal system. This would be a risky endeavor since half of the political elites of the country strongly support the current federal design. Any attempt to undo it would certainly lead to conflict if not war. The federal government would face resistance and opposition if attempts a top-down approach to redesign the federal system. The country thus finds itself in a political and constitutional quandary the way out of which is far from clear.

References

Afigbo, A. (1991). Background to Nigerian federalism: Federal features in the colonial state. *Publius: The Journal of Federalism, 12*(4), 13-29.

Anderson, D. M. (2005). 'Yours in Struggle for majimbo': Nationalism and the party politics of decolonization in Kenya, 1955-64. *Journal of Contemporary History, 40*(3), 547–564.

Bandyopadhyay, S., & Green, E. (2013). Nation-building and conflict in modern Africa. *World Development, 45*, 108-118.

Boon, C. (2012). Land Conflict and Distributive Politics in Kenya. *African Studies Review, 55*(1), 75-103.

Bosire, C. M. (2013). Devolution for development, conflict resolution, and limiting central power: An analysis of the Constitution of Kenya 2010 [*Unpublished PhD thesis*, University of Western Cape, Cape Town].

Duzor, M., & Williamson, B. (2023, October 3). *Coups in Africa*. Voice of America. Retrieved February 23, 2024, from https://projects.voanews.com/african-coups/

Erk, J. (2023). Lessons from the law and politics of federalism in Africa: Federalism is bigger than federation; constitutions are more than single mega-documents; the international trumps the domestic; and the past continues to matter. *Verfassung in Recht und Übersee, 56*(3), 633-654.

Fessha, Y., & Ayele, Z. (2021). Internal secession: The Ethiopian experience in comparative perspective. In M. Belov (Ed.), *Territorial politics: Constitutional and international law perspective* (pp. 265-287). Springer Nature, Cham.

Fessha, Y. (2010). *Ethnic diversity and federalism: Constitution-making in South Africa and Ethiopia*. Ashgate: Farnham.

Fessha, Y. (2017). The original sin of Ethiopian federalism. *Ethnopolitics, 16*(3), 232-245.

Gedlu, M. (1997). Democracy by order—Sub-Saharan Africa after the Cold War. *Perspectives, 9*, 97–107.

Kwatemba, S. W. (2008). Ethnicity and political pluralism in Kenya. *Journal of African Elections, 7*(2), 77-112.

Kadima, D., & Owuor, F. (2014). Kenya's decade of experiments with political party alliances and coalitions: Motivations, impact and prospects. *Journal of African Elections, 13*(1), 150-180.

Mnyongani, F. D. (2008). Between a rock and a hard place: The right to self-determination versus uti possidetis in Africa. *The Comparative and International Law Journal of Southern Africa, 41*(3), 463-479.

Nybira, M., & Ayele, Z. (2016). The state of political inclusion of ethnic communities under Kenya's devolved system. *Law Democracy and Development, 20*, 131-153.

Selassie, A. G. (2003). Ethnic federalism: Its promise and pitfalls for Africa. *Yale Journal of International Law, 28*, 51-107.

Statista. (2019). Distribution of the population of Kenya as of 2019, by ethnic group. Retrieved from https://www.statista.com/statistics/1199555/share-of-ethnic-groups-in-kenya/ (last accessed on 26 May 2024).

Suberu, R. T. (2023). Nigeria: A model of federalist ethnic conflict management or federalist illusion? In J. Kincaid, & L. Leckrone (Eds.), *Teaching federalism: Multidimensional approaches* (pp. 242–253). Edward Elgar Publishing Limited, Cheltenham.

Suberu, R. T. (2022). *Ethnic inequality, the federal character principle, and the reform of Nigeria's presidential federalism* (WIDER Working Paper 2022/113). UNU-WIDER.

Thomas, C. G., & Falola, T. (2020). *Secession and separatist conflicts in postcolonial Africa*. Calgary: University of Calgary Press.

Veenendaal, W., & Demarest, L. (2021). How population size affects power-sharing: A comparison of Nigeria and Suriname. *Contemporary Politics, 27*(3), 271-291.

Yimenu, B. (2024). Federalism and state restructuring in Africa: A comparative analysis of origins, rationales, and challenges. *Publius: The Journal of Federalism, 54*(1), 6-33.

9

IS DIVERSITY TURNING INTO DISUNITY IN BRAZIL?

Rogerio Schlegel

Introduction

Federalism represents the opportunity to achieve "diversity within unity" as proposed by many authors. The case of contemporary Brazil shows how tensions may stem from this general picture suggesting solidarity and togetherness, even in a country with limited historical cleavages regarding ethnicity, cultural traditions, and territorial identities. Recent episodes and emerging trends indicate that diversity may be evolving into disunity, in Elazarian terms, in the Brazilian Federation. Increasing polarization, particularly evident along territorial lines, poses significant challenge to the federal pact and may even exacerbate threats to democratic governance.

Brazil is usually considered a mono-national country marked by unity. There is a shared national identity that transcends regional divisions. Unity is evident in terms of identities, in the sense that there is a prevailing "brazilianness" that appeals to different ethnic and cultural groups. While significant territorial asymmetries exist, particularly concerning wealth and living standards, they are often accepted as given, as achieving full equalization among citizens from different subnational entities is not a primary national objective. Political forces advocating for equality usually target mitigation and shortening gaps rather than focusing on unbiased living conditions.

Nevertheless, some of these asymmetries can be – and actually have recently been – politically activated. The clearest evidence of such a process is the evolution of the voting pattern in presidential elections. As different parts of the globe, Brazil has recently witnessed a growing political polarization associated with the emergence of populist and extreme-right forces. This polarization has been increasingly expressed along territorial lines, opposing North and Northeast, regions concentrating votes for Luiz Inácio Lula da

Silva's party (PT), and South and Southeast, where most voted for right-wing candidates. This divide in attitudinal terms is already deeper than electoral results would suggest. With the emergence of the far-right in Brazil since the 2010s, the threat to democracy in Brazil is increasingly taking on the form of a federal issue.

This chapter provides historical information on the Brazilian federation, presents data on ethnic groups and territorial identities, and briefly discusses preferences regarding public policies. It then highlights how the electoral emergence of the extreme right might be associated with public policy outcomes, outlining a territorial divide in terms of political identities. As a final remark, it suggests a potential interplay between (the defense of) democratic governance and federal issues.

On notions of unity and diversity

Elazar (1987, pp. 64-66) argued that in federations unity and diversity should not be understood as polar opposites but rather as congruent concepts. The opposite of unity would not be diversity, but disunity. While the author did not thoroughly define what disunity means, it was outlined as something similar to conflict. Diversity would be the opposite of homogeneity and would manifest through nationality or ethnic, religious, ideological, and social dimensions. The essence of the federal idea would be that these two concepts can coexist comfortably to produce a particular kind of unity, federal unity. Let us set aside Elazar's axis related to unity-disunity at this point and focus on the other continuum. The notion of an axis of homogeneity-diversity might prove useful to understand Brazilian identities. Although the country is far from homogeneous, its diversity does not manifest as different nations or regions clamoring for devolution or secession. This framework allows us to think of a country where unity of identity prevails, yet there is significant diversity to be acknowledged.

Reviewing our nation and state-building processes is of paramount relevance to understanding our current standing on this matter. For those unfamiliar with Brazilian history, the following scheme, although as problematic as every periodization, may serve as a heuristic shortcut for the republican period:

- First Republic (1889-1930): Typically characterized as an oligarchic regime, with liberal institutions such as voting and separation of powers formally in place.

- Vargas Years (1930-1945): Named after the civilian leader of the 1930 Revolution, who established the *Estado Novo* ("New State") dictatorship (1937-1945) in a self-coup with military support.
- The so-called 1946 Democracy (1946-1964): Marked by competitive party politics and populist linkages to a growing mass electorate.
- Military Regime (1964-1985): Characterized by successive generals in power with support from civilian sectors.
- The ongoing democratic period: Dated either from the return of civilian rule to the Presidency (1985) or the promulgation of the most recent constitution (1988).

Many specialists in Brazil would describe this trajectory as marked by waves of centralization and decentralization in a pendular fashion. For instance, after Getulio Vargas' centralizing Dictatorship, the democratization of 1946 would have led to decentralization; then another period of centralizing authoritarianism came with the military, and so on. The supposed association of democracy and decentralization has inspired an influential metaphor to describe the trajectory of the Brazilian federation: the alternation of authoritarian and democratic regimes would have generated cycles of centralization and decentralization comparable to the regular "systoles and diastoles" of the cardiac muscle. However, a systematic assessment of this hypothesis revealed its clear oversimplification, which overshadows the contribution it might have to understanding the trajectory of the federation (Schlegel, 2023).

The recognition of centripetal and centrifugal forces prevailing at different points in time appears as a more useful starting point. Some key centripetal forces include: territorial unity, valued by political elites since monarchical times; faith in state-led economic development, which influenced government actions regardless of regime, from 1930 to at least the end of the 1970s; welfare policies initiated under the centralist government of Getulio Vargas, with path dependence effects that lasted until the 1988 Constitution; the role of the military, as they advocated for centralism throughout the 20th century.

As key centrifugal forces, one can mention: the need to accommodate asymmetric interests at the outset of the Republic; the territorial fragmentation of the multiparty system; and the association of democracy with decentralization at the end of the Military Regime in the 1980s.

Less clear is the role of the historical and pronounced territorial inequalities in terms of wealth, population, and political power. The country is marked by dramatic territorial asymmetries, with wealth and population concentrated in the South and Southeast regions [see also the chapter by Marta Arretche in this volume]. Political and social elites from poorer and less influential states have repeatedly joined pro-centralization coalitions as a means of counterbalancing the power of richer states and accessing more resources from the center. This has resulted in a persistent feature of the electoral system: São Paulo and other economically dynamic states have been underrepresented in the lower chamber of Congress since the Electoral Code of 1932 [see also the chapter by Cláudio Couto in this volume]. This type of malapportionment has survived two transitions to democracy (Nicolau, 1997). Redistributive issues are always a contentious topic in constitutional assemblies – the Brazilian federation has experienced three of them during its republican history – and other institutional reforms.

Unity above diversity

In terms of diversity, the country is fundamentally mono-national, with a dominant group espousing the national identity, but it contains considerable ethnic and cultural diversity due to colonization, slavery, and immigration. The country's population is ethnically diverse, with over 50% identifying themselves as Afro-Brazilians (*pretos* and *pardos*, expressions similar in meaning to black and brown), and almost 1% consisting of indigenous peoples.

Has it generated tensions within the federation, with cleavages or conflicts along territorial lines or secession claims? The short answer is no, but things might be changing. There is a growing sense of attachment among those who belong to groups previously considered as minorities. The group of individuals identifying themselves as black increased 32% in ten years (from 2012 to 2021), and there are 11% more people self-identifying as brown (IBGE, 2023). The proportion of blacks and browns is higher in the North and Northeast and lower in the South.

Regarding indigenous peoples, more than 50% of them live in the so-called legal Amazon, in northern states. The last national election saw a record of candidates self-declared as indigenous running for the House of Representatives (*Câmara dos Deputados*). There were 84 in 2014, 134 in 2018, and 175 in 2022 (Perobelli, Olivares, & Kelly, 2022). Five of them were elected among the 513 representatives – another record, following just one elected indigenous candidate in 2018. Four of them were elected in southeastern states.

The significance of the issues related to original peoples and environmental protection is also evident in the creation of the first-ever Ministry of Original Peoples during the third Lula Administration, inaugurated at the beginning of 2023. This was in response to the wave of violence and land invasions stimulated by Jair Bolsonaro's dismantling of the protection network for indigenous peoples. This issue intersects with populism and democratic backsliding, as well as the Climate Emergency. The demarcation of indigenous reserves poses an obstacle to the expansion of agribusiness and mining activities in the North of the country. Right-wing political parties close to Bolsonaro have vehemently opposed the acknowledgment of indigenous rights, particularly those related to land.

None of this seems to have unsettled the usual majoritarian convergence of Brazilian population around a national territorial identity. Using the Linz/Moreno question to gauge territorial attachment, Schlegel, Ferrari and Arretche (2023) revealed that the dual identity – the declared attachment to both the country and the state of residence at similar levels – prevailed during the 2010s[6]. Surveys conducted in 2013 and 2018 arrived at figures for dual identity higher than 45% in every region of Brazil. For comparison, Catalans showed 33% dual identity and 58% regional identity in 2016 (Guinjoan & Rodon, 2016); 34% of the English revealed dual identity against 40% who declared themselves English but not British in the beginning of the 2010s (Jones et al., 2012); in Belgium, around 42% manifested dual identity in Flanders and Wallonia, but in the former, national identity reached 31% and in the latter, 48% (Deschouwer et al., 2015).

The attachment exclusively to the states grew between 2013 and 2108 in every region, from 20% to 30% of the respondents, in round numbers. Brazil experienced a civil and political turmoil during these years, with massive street demonstrations (2013), the largest ever investigation of corruption among politicians known as the Car Wash Operation, which targeted main figures in the Worker's Party government and parties supporting its

---

[6] This question is likely to be the most employed measure of national and regional identity in public opinion research. In surveys, respondents are asked if they agree with a set of statements. For instance: from the pole "I feel Brazilian but not Paulista" (inhabitant from the state of São Paulo), passing through "I feel more Paulista than Brazilian", "I feel as Brazilian as Paulista", and the "I feel more Brazilian than Paulista", to the pole "I feel Paulista, but not Brazilian". Those who agree with the three alternatives in the middle are considered to have dual territorial identity.

administrations, the impeachment of the president Dilma Rousseff (2016), the inauguration of the former vice-president Michel Temer, and subsequent U-turn in various aspects of public policies and macroeconomic policy. The fieldwork for the second wave of the mentioned survey took place in 2018 before the election of Jair Bolsonaro and partially reflects the national mood at that point. Even the crisis of confidence brought about by these events was not enough to close the gap between the dual identity and regional identity – those who feel attached to their region only.

Apparently in line with this territorial identity, we found that in general Brazilians consider national decisions to be the most important, with subnational government's decisions lagging far behind. Brazilians also perceive national elections as the most important, with local-level elections even more relevant than those at the state level. Most Brazilians prefer homogenous policies throughout the territory. In our surveys, proportions higher than 60% of respondents believed that policies for poverty mitigation, tackling unemployment, providing unemployment insurance, promoting education, caring for the elderly, promoting healthcare, fixing the minimum wage, and setting pensions values should be the same throughout the country (Schlegel, Ferrari, & Arretche, 2023).

In sum, the institutional framework and the design of public policies thus far appear to be in line with citizens' preferences, at least at face value. Brazilians seem to support the cooperative approach the federation has employed in many policy areas, with legislative authority over most policies concentrated at the center. At the same time, the sense of "brazilianness" is still strong, despite being stronger a few years ago.

Diversity today, disunity tomorrow?

I have discussed above how the territorial identity has oscillated towards higher levels of regional identity. The territorial distribution of votes in presidential elections is another novelty pointing to potential changes regarding the political effects of diversity in the Brazilian federation. Since 2006, the country experienced a geographical divide in terms of votes for president. Until then, the winner tended to have their votes quite proportionally distributed across states. This was the case with Fernando Collor in 1989, Fernando Henrique Cardoso in 1994 and 1998, and with Lula in 2002. However, in 2006 and thereafter, the Workers' Party candidate – either Lula or Dilma Rousseff – concentrated votes in the states of the North and Northeast, while their opponent won in the Center-West, Southeast, and South. This was evident in the last election, in 2022, with Bolsonaro facing Lula in the second round.

A promising hypothesis to explain this trend is that the beginning of the differentiation between the two territorial blocs was initially generated by a compositional effect: once in power, Lula and the Workers' Party developed public policies that particularly favored low-income citizens. These voters were not evenly distributed throughout the country but were disproportionally concentrated in the Northeast and the North. Subsequent electoral choices might have reflected the favorable assessment of these policies by these poorer voters, creating a territorial divide. As this pattern has shown stability, there seems to be potential to this original compositional effect to evolve into an identity issue. The emergence of the extreme right may have associated with this process, outlining a growing territorial divide.

There has been some evidence in this direction:

- In 2018, the Workers' Party elected 4 governors and 5 allies out of nine northeastern states; in 2022, the party again elected 4 governors and 4 allies in the region.

- During the COVID-19 pandemic, governors of the Northeast created a consortium around health policies and were confronted by the Bolsonaro Administration and its negationist initiatives [see also the chapter by Eduardo Grin in this volume]. The confrontation through the media lasted until the end of his administration.

- The chief of the Brazilian Federal Police ordered special operations to supervise buses in the region on the day of the 2022 presidential election. Apparently, the idea was to create difficulties for Lula's voters getting to the polls.

- Demonstrations of prejudice by Bolsonaro voters against the Northeast and its population gained national media attention during the last presidential campaign.

These episodes suggest that the emergence of new layers of collective experiences may lead to enduring political stances and even have impact on territorial identities with political consequences. Polarization "can kill democracies", because deep social cleavages and acute political tensions can make ordinary people to compromise democratic principles for partisan interests (Levistky & Ziblatt, 2018; Slovik, 2019). In the case of Brazil, democracy has been a central issue in the polarization between extreme-right forces, represented by Bolsonaro, and those opposing authoritarianism, rallying around Lula in the most recent election (Filgueiras, Sena Jr., & Felipe Miguel, 2023). Could disunity develop in the form of territories more and less inclined to defend democracy?

Final remarks

In Brazil, the main territorial cleavages within the federation have revolved around income and wealth. Despite their significance to the functioning of the political realm, signs of enduring consequences of these features in terms of territorial identity used to be rare. An overarching sense of "brazilianness" has prevailed over ethnic and cultural diversity. Preferences regarding public policy also pointed to a desire for national homogeneity. The administrative design of the federation appears to align with this identity and with preferences for homogeneous policies.

Nevertheless, recent presidential elections have revealed polarization that is also expressed along territorial lines. It encompasses more than just electoral choices regarding policies, considering that defending or rejecting democracy has been a decisive factor in shaping this polarization. Some analysts argue that federalism can play a role in preserving democracy, but threats to democracy may also impact federal dynamics. The case of contemporary Brazil serves as a reminder that threats to democracy can intersect with federal issues, precisely because federations are political pacts that are continuously built and rebuilt.

References

Deschouwer, K. et al. (2015). Measuring (sub)national identities in surveys: Some lessons from Belgium. In *Proceedings of the Conference The State of the Federation* (Liège, Belgium, December 18, 2015). Université de Liège, Liège.

Elazar, D. (1987). *Exploring federalism.* Tuscaloosa: University of Alabama Press.

Fausto, B. (1994). *História do Brasil.* Editora da Universidade de São Paulo.

Filgueiras, L., Sena Júnior, C. Z. de, & Felipe Miguel, L. (2023). A eleição de 2022 e o seu significado. *Caderno CRH, 36,* e023023.

Gagnon, A., & Burgess, M. (Eds.). (2018). *Revisiting unity and diversity in federal systems of government*. Brill Press.

Guinjoan, M., & Rodon, T. (2016). A scrutiny of the Linz-Moreno question. *Publius: The Journal of Federalism, 46*(1).

Instituto Brasileiro de Geografia e Estatística (IBGE). (2023). Censo 2022: Pela primeira vez, desde 1991, a maior parte da população do Brasil se declara parda. *Agência IBGE Notícias*. Retrieved January 15, 2024, from https://agenciadenoticias.ibge.gov.br/agencia-noticias/2012-agencia-de-noticias/noticias/38719-censo-2022-pela-primeira-vez-desde-1991-a-maior-parte-da-populacao-do-brasil-se-declara-parda

Jones, R. W. et al. (2012). The dog that finally barked: England as an emerging political community. *Institute for Public Policy Research* (IPPR Report).

Levitsky, S., & Ziblatt, D. (2018). *How democracies die*. Ashland: Broadway Books.

Nicolau, J. M. (1997). As distorções na representação dos Estados na Câmara dos Deputados Brasileira. *Dados, 40*(3), 441-464.

Perobelli, A., Olivares, P., & Kelly, B. (2022). Número recorde de indígenas concorre ao Congresso em reação a Bolsonaro. *Reuters*. Retrieved January 15, 2024, from https://noticias.uol.com.br/ultimas-noticias/reuters/2022/09/22/numero-recorde-de-indigenas-concorre-ao-congresso-em-reacao-a-bolsonaro.htm

Schlegel, R. (2023). Dynamic de/centralization in Brazil, 1889–2020: The prevalence of punctuated centralization. *Regional & Federal Studies, 33*(5), 637-669.

Schlegel, R., Ferrari, D., & Arretche, M. (2023). As preferências do brasileiro sobre a federação. In P. Palotti, E. C. Licio, S. Gomes, C. I. Segatto, & A. L. N. da Silva (Eds.), *E os Estados? Federalismo, relações intergovernamentais e políticas públicas no Brasil contemporâneo*. Rio de Janeiro: Ipea.

Svolik, M. (2019). Polarization versus democracy. *Journal of Democracy, 30*(3), 20-32.

10

FEDERALISM AND RECENTRALIZATION: NEW TREND IN INTERGOVERNMENTAL RELATIONS? AN ACCOUNT FROM MEXICO

Juan C. Olmeda

Introduction

Since the beginning of the XXI century recentralization has gained momentum in many Latin American countries (Dickovick, 2011). In a sense, it was a reaction to a previous trend that was prominent during the '80s and the '90s: decentralization. Decentralization had come attached to many promises: to bring decision-making closer to the people, to make public officials more accountable, to promote participation at the local level, to make public spending more efficient (Montero & Samuels, 2004). Since most of those promises did not materialize, recentralization began to be conceived as a solution and became common in a diverse set of countries, both unitary and federal. Since recentralization is usually associated with attempts to concentrate power it is important to draw attention to the issue in order to discuss, address and better understand the effects of this phenomena both on the way in which political institutions work and on the prospects for democracy.

In this chapter, and in line with previous work on the subject (Olmeda & Armesto, 2017; Olmeda & Pérez Márquez, 2022), I analyze recentralizing reforms observed in Mexico during the last decades. First, I define what I understand when using the concept. Later, I briefly present the evolution of Mexican federalism, especially during the XX century. Finally, I focus on the main reforms observed in the country during the presidencies of Enrique Peña Nieto (2012-2018) and Andrés Manuel López Obrador (2018-2024).

Conceptualizing recentralization

In defining recentralization, I follow the conceptualization proposed by Eaton and Dickovick (2004, p. 94) who conceive this trend as "...a series of changes designed to reverse prior reforms that expanded subnational autonomy and thereby limited the prerogatives of the national government". Like previous decentralizing reforms (Falleti, 2010), recentralization might affect the political, fiscal and administrative spheres that regulate the relationship between levels of government (Dickovick, 2011). In addition, recentralizing policies might adopt different forms and re-shape particular policy areas. Dickovick and Eaton (2013) argue that it is possible to differentiate recentralization reforms that are explicit, in the sense that propose a redefinition of the legal framework that regulates the distribution of responsibilities, prerogatives and resources between the national and the subnational governments, from those that are more "subtle". The latter involve strategies adopted by the national government (i.e. the implementation of wide-scope national programs with territorial impact) that provide "...opportunities for the center to reclaim the role of protagonist that it often lost as a result of decentralization" without major legal reforms (Dickovick & Eaton, 2013, p. 1.454). In this case subnational autonomy is affected in an indirect way.

During the last decades of the XX century, decentralization was promoted as a way of achieving multiple goals at the same time. The transfer of responsibilities to subnational or local governments was expected to make public spending more efficient and government programs more attuned to citizens' real needs. At the same time, it would reduce the administrative burdens attached to decision making processes, avoiding the need that an official at the center would have the final say to solve problems that occurred at the local level. In addition, subnational or local authorities responsible for delivering public services in their territories would be more accountable for their decisions and be rewarded or punished for their results (Montero & Samuels, 2004)

Despite being conceived as a reversal of decentralization, recentralizing reforms did not pursue opposite goals. Recentralization did not attempt to make spending more inefficient, increase the complexity of bureaucratic procedures, or reduce accountability of subnational local officials. Certainly, it was perceived by national authorities as a way to redefine the balance of power in their favor. But it was also justified by the idea that decentralization had not fulfilled its promises and had produced more negative consequences than positive outcomes. However, an important consequence is that recentralization reduces subnational autonomy, and therefore affects the functioning of federal settings.

Like in the case of decentralization, recentralization can affect the administrative, fiscal and political spheres, involving reforms as a result of what the federal government regains power to design policies that were previously in the realm of subnational governments, create new taxes that are not shared with subnational units or implement some reforms that limit the room for political maneuver of subnational authorities.

Different works have proposed that the pair decentralization/recentralization should be understood in relation to issues such as regime type, political ideology and/or the incentives of national and subnational authorities (see Dardanelli et al., 2023; Eaton, 2013; Olmeda & Armesto, 2017). Regarding the first topic, decentralization has been thought as a way to strength democracy while recentralization has been linked to authoritarian settings. This relationship also implies that democratic governments will be more prone to decentralize while authoritarian ones will try to recentralize. In relation to the second issue, decentralization has been linked to the neoliberal agenda that adopted the principle of subsidiarity as a central pillar, while recentralization has been associated with the (neo) developmental approaches that propose that the state should assume a central role in the economy and providing social services and goods. Finally, it has been argued that subnational governments will favor decentralization and oppose recentralization while the incentives of national authorities are in the opposite direction.

In the next sections I focus on patterns observed in Mexico during the last decades to illustrate some of the points discussed so far.

The Mexican case: a brief background

Mexico was one of the first countries, after the United States, to adopt a federal model in the Constitution enacted in 1824 (Vazquez, 1993) However, the path to federalism was different in the Mexican case because it was an example of what Stepan (2004) has defined as "holding-together". In this first federal experience, that lasted only a few years, the states retained significant power. During the rest of the XIX century, in a context defined by internal and external conflicts, the federal model was re-enacted and later abandoned several times (Carmagnani, 1993). It was not until the last decades of that century when it was finally recovered once territorial integration and social stabilization were achieved. Federalism was indeed a central pillar of the 1917 Constitution that was enacted after the Mexican Revolution and is has remained in place until today.

During most of the XX century, however, Mexican federalism functioned in a very centralized way (Díaz Cayeros, 2006) This was the result of the existence of a hegemonic party system that for 7 decades dominated Mexican politics. Elections for legislative and executive positions were held on a regular basis at the national and subnational levels, but only the ruling party's candidates (the *Partido Revolucionario Institucional* PRI) were able to win. In this framework, Mexican presidents, who were also the main leaders of the ruling party, had always the final word in most issues (Hernández Rodriguez, 2008). Governors retained some autonomy, but they were able to exercise it only if their actions did not challenge presidential orders.

The situation began to change during the 1980s because of two main transformations that redefined the functioning of the federal model. The first one was democratization or the opening of the political system "from below" (Beer, 2003). The second was decentralization (Cabrero Mendoza, 1998; Ward & Rodriguez, 1999). In relation to the first issue, opposition parties began to win positions first at the municipal and later at the state level. In 1989 an opposition candidate won a governorship for the first time in decades in the state of Baja California. The same happened later in other states and even in Mexico City, the most important subnational unit in the country. Of course, these governors enrolled in the opposition began to confront with the president.

On the other hand, and as a result of increasing political pressures, the Mexican federal government pushed during those years for decentralizing reforms. These policies affected the administrative, fiscal and political spheres. Therefore, governors increased their control over resources (as a result of growing federal transfers) and their policy responsibilities, becoming more relevant players in Mexican politics (Hernández Rodriguez, 2008; Flamand, 2008).

The combination of these two trends reconfigured the balance of power between subnational units and the center. This change became even more clear once the PRI lost the presidential election in 2000 and when, a couple of years later, Mexican governors decided to create their own organization (the *Conferencia Nacional de Gobernadores* – CONAGO) to negotiate as a bloc with national authorities. Through the active role of this association, Mexican governors were able to obtain important benefits in the fiscal realm, which increased the portion of resources under their control (Olmeda, 2021).

These intertwined processes produced unanticipated negative consequences. First, some subnational political elites used their increased power to establish an authoritarian control in their states (Gibson, 2005; Giraudy, 2015). The consensus was that governors used public resources and the state apparatus to consolidate electoral machines and clientelist networks. In some cases, they even extended their influence over the legislative and judicial branches of government. Second, the heterogenous level of capacities of subnational administrations became even more clear, which had substantive effects in the quality of policy policies. Some states functioned in a very efficient way while with other states didn't function at all. In a historical unequal country like Mexico these differences had a substantive effect, especially when violence related to drug-trafficking increased. Third, the weak character of most subnational bureaucracies allowed for particular interests' groups and criminal organizations to co-opt some agencies and to use them for their own benefits. For example, it was well documented that in several states the subnational branches of the National Teachers´ Trade Union were able to have their representatives appointed at the top level in the states´ secretaries of education (Fernández, 2012) At due time, the organization used that influence to obtain resources, to control teachers' appointments and evaluations, and to have the final words in relation to the design and implementation of educational policies.

Recentralization as a backlash

Some of the problems described in previous paragraphs helped to put previous decentralization policies into question and recentralization began to be conceived as the unavoidable path to deal with the situation.[7] It is interesting that at that time it was not possible to look for other alternatives, such as working with state governments to improve their capacities. A new consensus around the idea of recentralizing faculties that had been previously transferred to the states and/or to push for national programs with territorial effects. The latter had been indeed a practice already in place

---

[7] Most of the issues discussed in this section are addressed in more detail in Olmeda and Armesto (2017) and Olmeda and Pérez Márquez (2022).

during the administrations of Vicente Fox (2000-2006) and Felipe Calderón (2006-2012) in areas such as poverty alleviation, security and education. During those years a "subtle" recentralization began to take form.

However, more explicit recentralization measures were adopted once Enrique Peña Nieto (2012-2018) took office and have continued during the presidency of Andrés Manuel López Obrador (2018-2024). Indeed, the "recentralizing consensus" remained in place despite the substantive ideological differences between López Obrador, center-left/developmentalist, and the previous presidents, center-right/neoliberal. These reforms affected the administrative, fiscal and political spheres. However, the changes were justified using different reasons. During the government of Peña Nieto, the main claim was that state governments made a very inefficient use of resources and that their administrations had been co-opted by interests groups that used that power in their own benefits. In the case of López Obrador the emphasis was on the idea that corruption was rampant at the subnational level and that nationally designed policies would help to reduce regional inequalities.

In both cases prevailed a deep distrust about subnational authorities even though most governorships were in hands of members of the ruling party. An important difference is that during the Peña Nieto´s government recentralization was the result of a broad agreement between the most important political parties at that time to push for an extensive agenda of legislative reforms. Certainly, the attempt to recentralize electoral responsibilities became part of the list of reforms as a consequence of demands by one of the main parties in the opposition. The scenario was different with López Obrador, when recentralization was part of an attempt to increase the power of the national executive branch. In the administrative sphere the most significant reforms affected the education, health care and security areas.

In the first case, an educational reform enacted during the first months of Peña Nieto presidency recentralized teachers' payroll and evaluation. This was the result of a diagnosis that criticized that subnational governments' teachers' appointments as being indeed controlled by the teachers' union local branches and that many of those who got new positions received a salary without working. Many of those prerogatives were absorbed by the National Institute for Evaluating Education (INEE), a federal agency with autonomy from the National Executive. Even when López Obrador promoted another extensive educational reform (that reversed many of the changes promoted by the previous president), the federal government retained control over teachers' payroll.

Continuity was even more clear in the security area. López Obrador was successful in creating a national military-police force, the Guardia Nacional, something that Peña Nieto had tried before but had not been able to. A similar pattern was observed in the health care area. While Peña Nieto pushed for the recentralization in the purchase of medicines to supply clinics and hospitals throughout Mexico, López Obrador promoted the creation of a federal agency responsible for controlling all medical services across the country, including those in charge of subnational governments. The federal government even began with the construction of a "mega drug store" to stock medicines for the whole health care system.

In the fiscal realm both governments tried to make a stricter use of the mechanisms under federal government control to audit how the federal transfers are spent at the subnational level.

Continuity between both administrations was also clear in the case of political recentralization. During Peña Nieto's presidency, his most prominent attempt in this area was a proposal arguing for the creation of a national electoral agency that would be in charge of organizing and supervising elections at the federal, state and municipal level. As a result, all state electoral agencies (one per each Mexican state) would disappear, and their functions would be absorbed by the newly created one. The new scheme would replace the one existing until then, with a federal electoral agency in charge of federal elections and state electoral agencies in charge of state and municipal elections. The ruling party pushed for the reform as part of a broader agreement with one of the main opposition parties that claimed that state electoral agencies were de facto controlled by governors and used to influence elections' results in their favor. The proposed transformation ended up being possible only in part. As a result of governors' strong disapproval state electoral agencies were not dissolved, even though some of their prerogatives were limited. Lopez Obrador also proposed an electoral reform during his administration that included, again, an attempt to close state electoral agencies. However, the proposal did not have enough support.

Another similarity was observed in the idea, pushed for by both presidents, of creating new positions in the federal bureaucracy in charge of coordinating the implementation of all federal programs in each state.

In the case of Peña Nieto this position was temporary created only for the state of Michoacán to deal with a crisis of violence in the region. When Lopez Obrador took office, a similar position was created permanently for each state. Even when in both cases the move was justified as a way to make federal interventions more efficient, in fact the changes had political implications. Given the high dependency of most states on federal resources, those who were appointed to occupy these positions became key players in the state political scene, almost as powerful as governors.

Conclusion

While decentralization was the common pattern observed around the world, and especially in Latin America, during the last decades of the XX century, recentralization became popular since the beginning of the 2000s. Reforms promoted by the central government to regain control over prerogatives and resources previously transferred to subnational units attempt to deal with some of the pitfalls or unaccomplished promised of decentralization.

Mexico was a particular example of this tendency, and different recentralizing reforms were implemented during the last decade, both by presidents Peña Nieto and López Obrador. Interestingly, both presidents embraced different ideologies and pushed for almost opposite agendas. However, recentralization appeared as a point of continuity given a shared conviction about the negative results produced by previous decentralization reforms.

Finishing, it is possible to conclude with three considerations that, inspired by the Mexican experience, open avenues for more comparative research.

The first is that recentralization it is not necessarily attached to a particular ideological view of the world and can happen in democratic times.

The second is that governors do not necessarily oppose recentralization when they consider that the costs of losing prerogatives are not higher than the benefits of the previous status quo. This might be particularly the case when they face administrative recentralizing reforms in areas (such as education, health care or security) that are difficult to deal with.

Finally, recentralization can produce different effects on the "center". Reforms promoted during Peña Nieto's presidency gave more power to federal agencies that were autonomous from the executive (Baez Caballero,

2018), like the National Electoral Institute or the National Institute for the Evaluation of Education. In the case of Lopez Obrador, it was the executive branch, and the presidency itself, which ended up more powerful.

References

Báez Caballero, O. (2018). Centralización por vías nuevas: La expansión de órganos autónomos con capacidades nacionales en México. *Revista Técnica sobre Rendición de Cuentas, 12,* 37-56.

Beer, C. (2003). *Electoral competition and institutional change in Mexico.* Notre Dame: Notre Dame University Press.

Cabrero Mendoza, E. (1998). *Las políticas descentralizadoras en México (1983-1993): Logros y desencantos.* CIDE-Miguel Ángel Porrúa.

Carmagnani, M. (1993). El federalismo liberal mexicano. In M. Carmagnani (Ed.), *Federalismos latinoamericanos: México, Brasil, Argentina* (pp. 877-902). El Colegio de México.

Dardanelli, P. et al. (2023). Authoritarianism, democracy and de/centralization in federations: What connections? *Regional & Federal Studies, 33*(5), 577-606.

Diaz-Cayeros, A. (2006). *Federalism, fiscal authority, and centralization in Latin America.* Cambridge: Cambridge University Press.

Dickovick, T., & Eaton, K. (2013). Latin America's resurgent centre: National government strategies after decentralisation. *Journal of Development Studies, 49*(11), 1453-1466.

Dickovick, T. (2011). *Decentralization and recentralization in the developing world: Comparative studies from Africa and Latin America.* Pennsylvania State University Press.

Eaton, K. (2013). The centralism of 'Twenty-First-Century Socialism': Recentralising politics in Venezuela, Ecuador and Bolivia. *Journal of Latin American Studies, 45*(3), 421-450.

Eaton, K., & Dickovick, J. T. (2004). The Politics of Re-Centralization in Argentina and Brazil. *Latin American Research Review, 39*(1), 90-122.

Falleti, T. (2010). *Decentralization and subnational politics in Latin America.* Cambridge: Cambridge University Press.

Fernández, M. (2012). From the streets to the classrooms: The politics of education spending in Mexico (*PhD Dissertation*). Durham: Duke University.

Flamand, L. (2008). The new role of subnational governments in the federal policy process: The case of democratic Mexico. In G. O'Donnell, J. S. Tulchin, & A. Varas (Eds.) with W. Stubits, *New voices in the study of democracy in Latin America* (pp. 79-118). Woodrow Wilson Center Reports on the Americas.

Gibson, E. (2005). Boundary control: Subnational authoritarianism in democratic countries. *World Politics, 58*(1), 101-132.

Giraudy, A. (2015). *Democrats and autocrats.* Oxford: Oxford University Press.

Hernández Rodríguez, R. (2008). *El centro dividido: La nueva autonomía de los gobernadores.* Ciudad de México: El Colegio de México.

Mendoza, E. C. (1998). *Las políticas descentralizadoras en México (1983-1993): Logros y desencantos.* CIDE-Miguel Angel Porrúa.

Montero, A., & Samuels, D. (Eds.) (2004). *Decentralization and democracy in Latin America.* Notre Dame University Press.

Olmeda, J. (2021). *¿La unión hace la fuerza? La acción colectiva de los gobernadores en Argentina, Brasil y México.* Ciudad de México: El Colegio de México.

Olmeda, J., & Armesto, A. (2017). La recentralización y los gobernadores: ¿Por qué no siempre se oponen? *Foro Internacional, 57*(1), 109-148.

Olmeda, J. C., & Márquez, C. P. (2022). ¿Continuidad en el cambio? La recentralización en México durante las presidencias de Peña Nieto (2012-2018) y López Obrador (2018-). *Desarrollo, Estado y Espacio, 1*(1).

Stepan, A. (2004). Toward a new comparative politics of federalism, multinationalism, and democracy: Beyond Rikerian federalism. In E. L. Gibson (Ed.), *Federalism and democracy in Latin America* (pp. 29-84). Baltimore: Johns Hopkins University Press.

Vázquez, J. (1993). El federalismo mexicano, 1823-1847. In M. Carmagnani (Ed.), *Federalismos latinoamericanos: México, Brasil, Argentina* (pp. 1-50). El Colegio de México.

Ward, P., & Rodriguez, V. (1999). New federalism, inter-governmental relations and co-governance in Mexico. *Journal of Latin American Studies, 31*(3), 673-710.

11

THE DILIGENCE AND RESILIENCE OF RECENTRALIZATION REFORMS IN BRAZIL

Daniel Arias Vazquez

Introduction

In Brazil, reforms in social policies implemented in the 1990s aimed to improve program designs and optimize available resources through new forms of financing and federal coordination. These institutional reforms facilitated intergovernmental cooperation, changes in the funding rules, and new incentives to local governments in order they take responsibility for expanding the offer of regulated policies according to the guidelines set by the federal government. After these reforms, several studies mobilize expressions such as "unbalanced cooperation" (Abrucio, 2005), "circumscribed autonomy" (Almeida, 2005), "federal supremacy" (Arretche, 2015), and "features of a centralized federalism" (Machado & Palotti, 2021) to describe the kind of intergovernmental relations in Brazil. But how did the country recentralize policy decision-making?

This chapter analyses institutional and federal aspects of the reforms in education and health policies, highlighting the mechanisms used and the necessary changes in the legal system. Among the regulatory mechanism used are the earmarking of revenues, the imposition of minimum limits of expenditure, the establishment of specific funds to finance the policy, conditional transfers to the provision of programs, setting national standards for the local implementation of these programs and the demand for municipal resources counterpart. To introduce these measures, changes were made to the legislation (constitutional amendments, supplementary laws and norms issued by the ministries), according to the necessary institutional framework to ensure the achievement of established goals.

The results shows that the federal coordination of these policies imposed conditions on the receipt of federal funds tied to the provision of selected programs, requiring that they be offered locally but under set centrally guidelines.

Institutional reforms and federal coordination: how Brazil recentralized policy decision making?

The 1988 Constitution provided a significant fiscal decentralization, either by broadening the tax base of subnational governments (especially the states) or by the increase in transfers to the states and especially the municipalities. However, the Constitution did not clearly define the precise division of responsibilities for the provision of social policies among spheres of government, as shared competences prevailed in most social sector policies (Lobo, 1995).

Thus, any federal entity was constitutionally authorized to implement programs in the areas of health, education, welfare, housing, and sanitation. Symmetrically, the powers shared did not ensure cooperation and coordinated action between the three levels of government (Arretche, 2004). According to Castro et al. (2009), this definition required a subsequent regulation by ordinary legislation and, while this had not happened, there were imbalances and controversies that persisted in the years after the promulgation of the Constitution. Shortly after the enactment of the 1988 Constitution, the Brazilian federation was characterized by the absence of a clear definition of responsibilities between levels of government (Serra & Afonso, 1999) and federal coordination of the decentralization process (Affonso, 1995).

The reforms implemented in the second half of the 1990s also introduced federal regulatory mechanisms that disciplined the allocation of resources and the provision of certain policies. Not to mention boosting the decentralization process of burden, especially in the social area.

The challenge for the reform agenda introduced in the second half of the 1990s was the establishment of mechanisms for federal regulation without changes in the political regime and the previously decentralized policy making. Dickovick (2011) stated that the recentralization processes in Latin America promoted institutional changes through a process of layering: new rules coexist with the distribution of competences defined in the previews process of decentralization. In Brazil, the successful strategies of the PSDB's (1995-2002) and PT's administrations (2003-2016) efficiently explored the potential of these incentives to foster cooperation (Schlegel & Vazquez, 2021).

The objective was to improve the design of programs and optimize the resources that were already available for municipalities through new forms of funding and federal coordination. Another target was to establish a national performance standard capable of reducing horizontal inequalities in the resources available and the supply conditions of social policies.

Inserted into a political agenda and an international theoretical debate on the State Reform, these institutional reforms, also known as second generation reforms, aimed to enhance the action of the state and improve the effectiveness and the efficiency of social policies. In its broadest sense, this reform agenda aimed to build a new state regulation on the market, from the recovery of the regulatory capacity of the State, which implies the strengthening of institutions, with the definition of rules and incentives for cooperation between economic agents in the market and to better public management to driving development (Kuczynski & Williamson, 2003; Stiglitz, 1999). This setting can be easily adapted to explain the importance of institutions for federative coordination in Brazil because they dictate rules and put incentives that influence the decision of the local rulers toward an expected behavior, under guidelines set by the federal government.

Whether the institutional reforms represented radical transformation in federalism defined in 1988 (Melo, 2005) or consolidate a regulatory power already given to the Union by the Constitution (Arretche, 2009), there was actually a practical change in intergovernmental relations after 1995, when the decision-making autonomy of subnational governments began to be affected by rules and incentives set by the federal government, which did not exist before these reforms.

Thus, the challenge here is to analyze how these changes were put in place by the introduction of various institutional mechanisms that produced incentives for local governments to foster cooperation. The implementation of the reforms required the construction of different strategies to ensure the expansion of the measures' effectiveness and the accession of sub-national governments involved. Particular attention was paid for the specificities of each type of policy, such as the share of each level of government in their provision and financing. The legacy of political influence was also considered in the formulation of reforms, because only then it would be possible to generate the right incentives for the adhesion of local governments (Vazquez, 2012).

Therefore, the first step was to define what should be the degree of change required in law enforcement for the implementation of new regulatory mechanisms. For example, for the creation of the maintenance funds for the development of education (Fundef/Fundeb), and to establish the assignment of revenues for health financing were necessary Constitutional Amendments (EC), because these are the legal and institutional instruments required to change the standard financing of decentralized policies when these are borne primarily by resources already available to subnational governments.

When policies were locally executed and with significant funding from the federal budget — as in primary health care — new rules were defined counting on ministerial orders (ordinances, manuals, rules for transfers). Funds would only be transferred in case the nationally fixed criteria for provision are respected and, therefore, the central government can obtain the cooperation of municipalities and establish a national standard for the programs' supply.

The second step is to define the instruments used for federal coordination and for the induction of municipal governments towards the expected behavior, which should also be suitable for the type and characteristics of policy analysis. Among the range of these mechanisms, three types that are present in the reforms implemented in the education and health policies stood out: earmarking of revenues; specific funds; and conditional transfers. They are briefly described below.

Earmarking of revenues

The educational sector had already secured funds of the three levels of government before the 1988 Constitution through the Calmon Amendment of 1983. From 2000 onwards, the health sector could rely on earmarked state and local resources through Constitutional Amendment 29, aimed at increasing subnational participation in these areas and attracting the necessary resources for municipal contributions to the funding of primary health care programs.

This type of regulatory instrument can be considered the one with greatest capacity to intervene in the spending decisions of governments. According to Mendes (2003, p. 11), earmarking, on the one hand, "induces sub-national governments to increase their investments in a kind of public service as a national priority; on the other hand, it decreases the degrees of freedom that the city manager has to decide on the allocation of resources". Consequently, the spending decisions of local governments would be less driven by autonomous initiative and more by legal regulations regarding conditions for spending, such as 25% of revenues to education and 15% to health. With the recentralizing reforms, in addition to spending percentages, the Constitution and specific laws defined in more detail mandatory expenditures, such as allocating 15% of total resources for education to primary education; allocating at least 60% to teacher salaries; and funds conditional to primary health care services supply, preventive health campaigns, and the distribution of certain medicines (Arretche, 2004).

This mechanism tightened the link between locally levied revenues and spending, making the level of inequality in resources available for a given social policy more dependent on the local tax base than on government decisions.

Specific Funds

Policy-focused funds are composed of revenues of the three spheres of government to finance a specific social program. The redistribution of these resources is typically based on the effective provision of services or the proportion of potential beneficiaries within the state or municipality.

This mechanism promotes the redistribution of resources among subnational governments and represents advances in decentralization processes regarding policymaking. At the same time, it represents a coordination mechanism that explore the allocation of decentralized resources, as the targets of the policies are defined by the federal government (Almeida, 2005; Abrucio, 2005). These funds reinforce the central government's power in terms of policy decision-making.

The funds created to guarantee resources for primary education (Fundef, in 1996) and for primary and secondary education (Fundeb, in 2006) are exemplary cases. Both are formed with fiscal resources from the state and municipal governments, which they receive back according to the enrollment in public schools, based on a single value per student in each state of the federation, with supplementation of federal resources only when a minimum amount, defined nationally, is not reached. Thus, it is expected that horizontal inequalities decrease significantly after this redistributive effect, and the additional resources for each enrollment reduce the resistance of local governments to increase the provision of this policy.

Conditional Transfers

The significance of these transfers in Brazil increased during the second half of the 1990s, highlighting their crucial role in federal coordination. According to Prado (2007), this type of intergovernmental transfer reflects an effort to achieve national objectives in areas that are defined by the Constitution as typically subnational responsibility or of shared competence.

In addition to filling the vertical gap, this kind of transfer depends on the adhesion to certain programs, the compliance to centrally defined standards, and counterparts by subnational governments. Thus, the conditions imposed for the transfers affect the allocative decisions and restrict the budgetary autonomy of the subnational governments.

In short, conditional transfers in Brazil enable the transfer of funds to municipalities, based on redistributive criteria (population, for example) and/or each funded program own criteria (as in the case of the Family Health Program) and, therefore, it is expected that these transfers also collaborate with the reduction of horizontal inequalities in health financing.

Table 1 synthesizes the institutional mechanisms of federative coordination employed in the recent wave of recentralization. The synthesis focuses on policy rather than control instruments because different instruments are applied within the same policy. For example, education relies on decentralized revenue links and specific funds, while health also utilizes links, but the funding is comprised of federal funds transferred to municipalities via conditional grants, as outlined below.

Table 1. Federal regulation / Federal Coordination, by area

Field	Institutional Refoms	Legal and Institutional Planning	Cases
Basic Education	• Revenue earmarking of the three levels of government. • Multi-governmental funds with states' and municipalities' revenues. • Transfers proportional to provision of service.	• Constitutional Amendments • Complentary and Ordinary Laws	Fundef/ Fundeb
Primary Health Care	• Federal transfers conditioned to specific programs. • Linking of states and municipal revenues.	• Basic Operational Standards from the Ministry of Health. • Constitutional Amendment (only for linking).	Family Health Program

Source: Author's elaboration

It is important to note that this is not a single control strategy applied in different areas of government action. According to Vazquez (2012, p. 96), each regulatory instrument introduced "considered the specificities and the legacy of the policies in issues regarding skills for financing and implementation". They also took into account the necessity for supply expansion, the production of incentives for decentralization, and the introduction of mechanisms for redistribution of national resources and compatibility between decentralized revenue and local provision of public services.

Hence the importance of evaluating the effectiveness of federal coordination instruments and the results obtained in each area, as well as being able to subsidize any corrections of these mechanisms, considering that these experiences can be the basis for the construction of new regulations to policies hitherto unregulated, considering their specificities.

Conclusion

In Brazil, achieving federal coordination required obtaining the adherence of municipal governments to take over the provision of policies under centrally defined guidelines. Correct incentives had to be provided, addressing the interests of local governments and being appropriate to the institutional framework of each policy, considering the distribution of original jurisdiction, the responsibilities of each level in financing, and the existence of previous rules (path dependence). Through various legal and institutional mechanisms tailored to each area, policy reforms of the 1990s and 2000s promoted changes in the funding rules, conditioning transfers related to programs identified as priorities.

As a result, subnational governments could rely on an additional and reliable source of resources that would be available only if their officials chose to take the offer of selected programs and in a manner determined by the federal government. In basic education, financing and provision were predominantly decentralized, with revenue availability tied to the supply through the formation of funds comprising earmarked revenues from states and municipalities. A Constitutional Amendment stipulated that the redistributed resources in each unit of the Federation would reflect the proportion of students enrolled in its school system. In contrast, in health, the primary health care policy implementation was decentralized, but funding relied heavily on conditional transfers from the Union (via the Unified

Health System - SUS), and thus, the alignment of revenue and program provision was achieved through conditional transfers standardized by ministerial orders. The resources of the education funds and the conditioned transfers of SUS began to be allocated based on specific policy criteria, independently of each municipality's tax capacity. This earmarking of resources was useful in defining a minimum percentage of the budget to be spent by all municipalities in certain areas, regardless of the decision of local governments.

The recentralization of the 1990s and 2000s has shown some resilience. In both policy areas, renewed federal regulations are still in place. Even when challenged by the Bolsonaro government, whose concepts of federation can be considered rudimentary from a political design perspective (Vazquez & Schlegel, 2022), the institutional arrangement of Brazilian federalism remained intact. There is a growing consensus indicating that a lack of federative coordination characterized Bolsonaro's administration, as indicated by Abrucio et al. (2020) and Vazquez and Schlegel (2022). Although this period is outside the scope of this chapter, there are signs that this continuity is due to the recentralization process in Brazilian federalism, marked by the federal regulation (centralized policy decision-making) of locally implemented social policies (decentralized policymaking).

References

Abrucio, F. L. (2005). Coordenação Federativa no Brasil: A Experiência do Período FHC e os Desafios do Governo Lula. *Revista de Sociologia e Política, 24*, 41-67.

Abrucio, F. L. et al. (2020). Combating COVID-19 under Bolsonaro's federalism: a case of intergovernmental incoordination. *Revista de Administração Pública, 54*(4), 663-677.

Affonso, R. de B. Á. (1995). A Federação no Brasil: Impasses e Perspectivas. In R. B. Affonso, & P. L. B. Silva (Ed.), A *Federação em Perspectiva: Ensaios Selecionados* (pp. 57-76). FUNDAP.

Almeida, M. H. T. (2005). Recentralizando a Federação? *Revista de Sociologia e Política, 24*, 29-40.

Arretche, M. (2004). Federalismo e Políticas Sociais no Brasil: Problemas de Coordenação e Autonomia. *São Paulo em Perspectiva, 18*(2), 17-26.

Arretche, M. (2009). Continuidades e Descontinuidades da Federação Brasileira: De como 1988 Facilitou 1995. *DADOS – Revista de Ciências Sociais, 52*(2), 377-423.

Arretche, M. (2015). Intergovernmental relations in Brazil: an unequal federation with symmetrical arrangements. In J. Poirier, C. Saunders, & J. Kincaid (Eds.), *Intergovernmental Relations in Federal Systems: Comparative Structures and Dynamics* (pp. 108-134). Oxford: Oxford University Press.

Castro, J. A. et al. (2009). A CF/88 e as Políticas Sociais Brasileiras. In J. C. Cardoso Jr. (Ed.), *A Constituição Brasileira de 1988 Revisitada: Recuperação Histórica e Desafios Atuais das Políticas Públicas nas Áreas Econômica e Social* (pp. 55-122). Rio de Janeiro: Ipea.

Dickovick, J. T (2011). Recentralization in Latin America: institutional layering and presidential leverage. Proceedings of the *107th American Political Science Association's Annual Meeting, USA*. Retrieved from https://papers.ssrn.com/sol3/papers.cfm?abstract_id=1902939

Kuczyinski, P. P. & Williamson, J. (2003). *After the Washington Consensus: Restarting Growth and Reform in Latin America.* Peterson Institute for International Economics.

Lobo, T. (1995). Distribuição de Encargos na Área Social. In R. B. A. Affonso, & P. L. B. Silva (Eds.), A *Federação em Perspectiva: Ensaios Selecionados* (pp. 305-314). FUNDAP.

Machado, J. A. & Palotti, P. L.M (2015). Entre cooperação e centralização: federalismo e políticas sociais no Brasil pós-1988. *Revista Brasileira de Ciências Sociais, 88*(30), 61-82.

Melo, M. A. (2005). O Sucesso Inesperado das Reformas de Segunda Geração: Federalismo, Reformas Constitucionais e Política Social. *DADOS – Revista de Ciências Sociais, 48*(4), 445-489.

Mendes, M. J. (2003). A Eficácia da Vinculação de Recursos no Federalismo Brasileiro: O Caso do FUNDEF. In Secretaria do Tesouro Nacional, *Finanças Públicas* (pp. 275-330). Brasília: Editora da UnB.

Prado, S. (2007). *A Questão Fiscal na Federação Brasileira: Diagnósticos e Alternativas.* Rio de Janeiro: Ipea/CEPAL.

Schlegel, R. (2022). Dynamic de/centralization in Brazil, 1889–2020: The prevalence of punctuated centralization. Regional & Federal Studies, first online.

Serra, J. & Afonso, J. R. (1999). The Fiscal Federalism to the Brazilian: Some Reflections. *International Conference on Federalism – Forum of Federations*. Retrieved from https://www.forumfed.org/libdocs/IntConfFed99/ICFE9910-br-Serra-and-Afonso.pdf

Schelegel, R. & Vazquez, D. A. (2021). Coercion in Disguise? A Reassessment of Brazilian Education and Health Reforms. *Journal of Politics in Latin America, 13*(2), 243-268.

Stiglitz, J. (1999). More instruments and broader goals: moving toward the Post-Washington Consensus. *Brazilian Journal of Political Economy, 19*(1), 101-128.

Vazquez, D. A. (2012). *Execução Local sob Regulação Federal: Impactos da LRF, Fundef e SUS nos Municípios Brasileiros*. Annablume, FAPESP.

Vazquez, D. A., & Schlegel, R. (2022). Covid-19, Fundeb e o populismo do governo Bolsonaro nas relações federativas. *Revista Brasileira de Ciência Política, 38*, 1-32.

MANAGING INTERDEPENDENCIES IN FEDERAL SYSTEMS

Johanna Schnabel

Introduction

In federal systems, powers are divided between two (sometimes three) orders of government whose existence and autonomy are constitutionally entrenched (Fenna & Schnabel, 2023) [see also chapter by Alan Fenna in this volume]. Although federalism means division of powers and territorial autonomy, the federal government and the constituent units (and local governments) are hardly independent from each other in exercising their powers. Some interdependencies are typically built into the political system while others evolve through federal practice. Given the many interdependencies between the governments of a federation, intergovernmental relations (IGR) are a 'ubiquitous' (Poirier & Saunders, 2015a, p. 1) feature of federal systems, being the main mechanisms through which governments exchange information, pool resources, and coordinate policymaking.

This chapter presents different types of interdependencies in federal system; reviews the mechanisms and purpose of intergovernmental relations; and discusses a few issues concerning their operation. The conclusion identifies three models of intergovernmental relations. Rather than serving as a clear "template", these observations should be considered in light of the specific context, purpose, and challenges of a given federation.

Formal and informal interdependencies

Interdependencies can be built into the federal system in the form of shared powers or a functional division of powers where the constituent units implement federal legislation (Bolleyer & Thorlakson, 2012; Mueller & Fenna, 2022). Both mean that the two orders of government occupy a policy field, either because they are responsible for different aspects of it (shared powers) or because the federal government designs the policy and the constituent units deliver it (functional division of powers, or administrative federalism). Co-determination of federal legislation, a prominent feature of German federalism (Auel, 2014; Hegele, 2018), is another way of institutionalizing interdependence. Formal interdependencies can also exist among the constituent units, namely when federal law or the constitution mandate horizontal coordination. Education policy in Switzerland is a case in point (Fischer, Sciarini, & Traber, 2010).

Besides institutionalized interdependence, there are many other aspects that make governments mutually dependent. When policy problems cut across jurisdictions assigned to different orders of government, for instance, neither the federal government nor the constituent units can address them effectively and efficiently on their own (Hueglin & Fenna, 2015; Schnabel, 2020). Governments can also be interdependent because of fiscal dependence. Due to vertical fiscal imbalances, in particular, constituent units often rely on federal government transfers (Boadway & Shah, 2009; Cottarelli & Guerguil, 2015, p. 3). Negative or positive externalities increase the interdependence among the constituent units, encouraging coordination to foster the effectiveness and efficiency of policymaking (Oates, 1999, p. 1131). Formal and informal interdependencies exist, in one way or another, in all federations.

Intergovernmental relations

In response to the many interdependencies between governments, mechanisms of intergovernmental relations developed in all federations (and quasi-federations) (see Poirier, Saunders, & Kincaid, 2015). The term "intergovernmental relations" may be misleading due to its vagueness but has come to be used to describe a range of legislative and executive mechanisms through which the governments of a federation interact to exchange information, pool resources, or coordinate policymaking. Indeed, intergovernmental relations are 'the workhorse of any federal system' (Cameron, 2001, p. 121). Although Poirier and Saunders (2015a, p. 1) claim that they are an 'underappreciated' feature, their importance in the practice of federalism is widely acknowledged (e.g., Hueglin & Fenna, 2015, chap. 9; Osaghae, 2015; Mendoza Ruiz & Grin, 2020; OECD, 2020; Popelier, 2021; Ayele & Fessha, 2022).

However, it is important to highlight that although intergovernmental relations exist in all federations, they are not what makes a country federal. Federalism is about autonomy and intergovernmental relations exist because autonomous governments have to manage their interdependencies (Fenna & Schnabel, 2023). But federations are not formed for the sake of intergovernmental relations. This being said, intergovernmental relations can foster "federal success"; though what federal success means is open to debate and contingent on the specific context, the challenges of a given country, and citizens perceptions of it. There usually is a reason why a country is federal, meaning that federalism is expected to deliver something. Intergovernmental relations can help federalism fulfil this purpose and can be part of several safeguards of federalism (Bednar, 2009; Schnabel, 2020).

Whether intergovernmental relations enhance federal robustness and foster efficient and effective policymaking depends on a range of factors, including not least the political will of those actors involved. In particular, intergovernmental relations depend on the political will of the federal government to engage in coordination with the constituent units in a collaborative manner; although commitment by the constituent units, of course, is also a crucial factor. Intergovernmental relations are shaped by political parties (Bolleyer, 2011; Esselment, 2012); the pressures and challenges to which they have to respond (Braun, Ruiz-Palmero, & Schnabel, 2017); and the constitutional design of a country. For instance, countries with a high degree of interdependencies in the institutional setup, such as Germany and Switzerland, tend to have more developed intergovernmental relations (Hegele & Behnke, 2017; Schnabel & Mueller, 2017). Power sharing executive-legislative relations in consociational federations are also more conducive to institutionalization of intergovernmental relations than power separation and majoritarian dynamics (Bolleyer, 2006).

Intergovernmental relations usually involve the federal government and the constituent units (vertical IGR) to exchange information and coordinate policymaking across orders of government. In many cases, the constituent units also coordinate among themselves (horizontal IGR) to jointly address policy problems falling within their (exclusive) jurisdiction; fend off federal government intervention; or build leverage vis-à-vis the federal government (Papillon & Simeon, 2004; Nugent, 2009; Füglister & Wasserfallen, 2014; Hegele & Behnke, 2017).

Legislative mechanisms of IGR include bicameralism [see the chapter by Antonios Souris in this volume] and interparliamentary meetings (see also Bolleyer, 2010). Further mechanisms are framework legislation, which exists in some federations (e.g., Brazil, Spain), and the drafting of model laws, an instrument mainly used in the United States. Executive mechanisms include intergovernmental agreements, which are (often non-binding) treaties between governments. Governments can also establish joint bodies. The Australian Curriculum, Assessment, and Reporting Authority (ACARA), for instance, is co-funded by the federal government and the states and is responsible for developing a national curriculum and reporting on schooling on their behalf. Consultation requirements are another type of executive mechanism through which governments exchange information and coordinate policy. Article 45 of the Swiss constitution, for instance, requires the federal government to consult the cantons before passing legislation that affects their interest. This is done through highly formalized consultation procedures.

Finally, intergovernmental councils are the most important and most visible mechanism of intergovernmental relations (Bolleyer, 2009; Behnke & Mueller, 2017; Hegele & Behnke, 2017; Leon, 2017; Phillimore & Fenna, 2017; Schnabel & Mueller, 2017; Simmons, 2017). Intergovernmental councils are more or less regular meetings of members of government to discuss policy issues of joint concern. While meetings can be limited to information exchange, councils may also use issue statements; adopt resolutions; or sign intergovernmental agreements. Council outputs usually are not legally binding (Poirier, Saunders, & Kincaid, 2015), gaining legal status only if they lead to the passage of legislation or executive orders, but they can be politically binding.

Prominent examples of intergovernmental councils are First Ministers' Meetings and the Council of the Federation in Canada; the Conference of Minister-Presidents in Germany, National Cabinet (previously known as the Council of Australian Governments; COAG) in Australia; the Conference of Presidents in Spain; and the recently established Federation Council (*Conselho da Federação*) in Brazil. These are peak councils whose members are the political leaders of governments or entire governments (e.g., the Conference of Cantonal Governments in Switzerland). They tend to address highly political, cross-sectoral policy problems (Schnabel, Freiburghaus, & Hegele, 2022). Alongside them there typically exist a number of sectoral councils that tend to focus on policy-specific, less politicized issues. Some councils include the federal government (vertical councils), while others are only forums of the constituent units (horizontal councils). In most federations, including Argentina, Australia, Ethiopia, India, and Spain, all councils are vertical forums, while a few federations (notably Austria and Switzerland) only have horizontal councils. In other federations, for instance Canada, Germany, and Nigeria (Osaghae, 2015, p. 282), there are vertical *and* horizontal councils.

As Behnke and Mueller (2017) highlight, intergovernmental councils usually fulfil one or several of the following purposes: autonomy protection, influence, coordination, and information exchange. Those can be top down when initiated by the federal government or bottom-up when driven by the constituent units. Individual councils may fulfil different purposes or fulfil the purposes to a different extent. Nevertheless, there are certain cross-country patterns. For instance, councils in Australia and Canada pursue all three purposes and are dominated by the federal government while in Germany, intergovernmental councils largely focus on (top down and bottom-up) coordination and information exchange, leaving influence and autonomy protection to the second chamber, the *Bundesrat* (Hegele & Behnke, 2017, p. 544).

Intergovernmental relations and "federal success"

How do intergovernmental relations influence the outcomes of federalism? There are two sides to consider. On the one hand, intergovernmental relations can lead to better outcomes by promoting efficiency, effectiveness, and equity in policy making; for instance, when governments pool resources, agree on national standards, or harmonize policy making. Federalism is the "search for a (perpetually contested) optimal balance between autonomy and cohesion" (Popelier, 2021, p. 5). Cohesion is usually what the federal government exists for. However, intergovernmental relations can also foster cohesion and, in this way, offer an alternative to centralization.

On the other hand, intergovernmental relations tend to be highly complex and involve a multitude of actors. This can slow down decision making and generate blockage (Scharpf, 2008). Intergovernmental relations, due to their executive nature, can also undermine transparency, accountability, and parliamentary scrutiny, typically operating behind closed doors. All this may generate frustration among those federalism is supposed to serve as well as the actors involved in intergovernmental relations. Indeed, intergovernmental relations can increase the workload of public officials and complicate the participation of governments with low administrative capacity.

It is important to keep in mind that intergovernmental relations are not an end in itself. Intergovernmental information exchange, pooling of resources, and coordination should occur whenever there is a real benefit. When intergovernmental meetings occur only due to habit or rigid institutional constraint, they can become a threat to the autonomy of governments, and thus to the essential feature of federalism. If intergovernmental relations are too constraining and rigid, governments cannot be responsive to local circumstances and demands.

Issues in intergovernmental relations

There are several issues that are important to consider when thinking about how to design and make intergovernmental relations work. The first issue concerns the degree of institutionalization. Institutionalization is associated with reliability and continuity in the conduct of intergovernmental relations (Scharpf, 1988, p. 257; Bolleyer, 2009, pp. 21–25). It also facilitates a genuine partnership between orders of governments, making coordination more collaborative (Schnabel, 2020). It reduces the impact of changes in government. Low institutionalization makes intergovernmental relations more dependent on political will, momentarily overlapping interests, or external pressure.

According to Phillimore and Fenna (Phillimore & Fenna, 2017, p. 602), Australia's peak council, previously known as COAG and now called National Cabinet 'is, in the main, simply the occasional summit of first ministers from across Australia rather than an "institution" in any meaningful sense'. Does this suggest that COAG/National Cabinet does not actually exist? When meetings are called there is a certain expectation that first ministers will attend; they do indeed participate or at least send a representative. The council has a website and issues press releases reporting 'National Cabinet met…' and 'National Cabinet agreed…' The implementation of agreements at council meetings is sometimes monitored. All this suggests that the council does exist and that it generates some ongoing intergovernmental relations. This being said, COAG as well as its successor, National Cabinet, are weakly institutionalized. Other councils have a much more regular and frequent meetings, a permanent and independent secretariat, several committees, and a statute, which all foster the reliability and continuity of intergovernmental coordination.

At the same time, Simmons (2004) finds in a study on Canada that institutionalization does not influence compromising and consensus building. What is more, institutionalization may generate "rigidity", delay decision making and increase the workload of the officials, thus enhancing the downsides of intergovernmental relations. More complexity and rigidity may undermine the flexibility required to address current challenges. This raises the question whether, at least in some situations, informality may be 'better'.

The second issue concerns the role of the federal government. There is evidence that hierarchical coordination (Scharpf, 1994, p. 30; 1997), i.e., top-down steering by the federal government, may foster efficiency and effectiveness in intergovernmental relations and facilitate faster policy response in situations in which governments are interdependent. At the same time, hierarchical coordination can be ignorant towards local conditions and preferences. It can mean that the federal government imposes policy on the constituent units without considering their preferences, needs, and ability (or willingness) to implement a policy. The federal government imposing policy on the constituent units and coercing them to implement it undermines federalism, which is about territorial autonomy and is not a principal-agent arrangement. As mentioned above, in most federations, intergovernmental councils include the federal government. The federal government typically is not an equal member, being the chair of these vertical councils and providing their secretariat. This is not only the case in Australia's National Cabinet. First Ministers' Meetings in Canada, the Conference of Presidents in Spain, or Belgium's Concertation Committee are also led by the federal government, as are many sectoral councils in those and many other federations. This allows the federal government to exert significant influence on the intergovernmental agenda and dominate negotiations (Painter, 2001; Trench, 2006; Jensen, Koop, & Tatham, 2014; Poirier & Saunders, 2015b, pp. 459, 465), leading to intergovernmental friction and resistance and pushback by constituent units.

A final issue concerning the operation of intergovernmental relations refers to the role of the peak council. As mentioned above, in most federations there is a generalist council of the political leaders of governments or entire governments that tends to addresses cross-sectoral, highly politicized matters and that is at the apex of the council system. To what extent does this council play a leading role in intergovernmental relations and ensure cross-sectoral coordination in addition to coordination across jurisdictions? A study comparing the peak councils in Germany (the Conference of Minister-Presidents) and Switzerland (the Conference of Cantonal Governments) before and during the Covid-19 pandemic shows that these councils do not play a leading role in normal times (Schnabel, Freiburghaus, & Hegele, 2022). Due to the cross-sectoral and cross-jurisdictional character of crisis management and given the consequential decisions it involved, the Conference of Minister-Presidents assumed leadership during the Covid-19 pandemic, however. Similarly, National Cabinet in Australia was particularly active during the pandemic and was the main mechanism through which the federal government and states coordinated crisis management (Fenna, 2021). The Conference of Cantonal Governments did not take a leading role during the pandemic, and neither did the First Ministers' Meetings in Canada, suggesting that cross-sectoral coordination occurred elsewhere or did not occur *tout court*.

Conclusions

What insights can be gained from this overview of the mechanisms of intergovernmental relations, their purpose, and the three main issues outlined in the previous section? *In lieu* of a conclusion, this section describes three models of intergovernmental relations which combine empirical and theoretical insights.

The first model describes intergovernmental relations as a *partnership* between governments. In this model, intergovernmental councils have a rotating chair and independent secretariat, instead of being dominated by the federal government. Intergovernmental coordination is supported by several committees that prepare and revise recommendations. Another characteristic is the existence of different types of intergovernmental council, vertical and horizontal ones as well as generalist and sectoral councils. These councils are highly institutionalized but allow for flexibility to respond to urgencies. Typically, such collaborative intergovernmental relations are supported by constitutional design with strong safeguards of constituent unit autonomy, political will to cooperate as partners, and, very importantly, a long tradition of intergovernmental relations.

The second model is one where intergovernmental relations rely on hierarchical coordination. Hence, there is a strong federal government, and coordination occurs primarily in a top-down manner. The federal government chairs council meetings and provides their secretariat. In this model, the federal government uses intergovernmental relations and its spending power to offer financial incentives and coerce the constituent units into supporting its policy agenda (Watts, 1999; Fenna, 2008). Intergovernmental councils serve the federal government to monitor implementation and compliance of constituent units. This model does not do full justice to the idea of federalism, turning intergovernmental relations into a principal-agent arrangement. However, it may respond to certain needs in post-conflict societies and holding-together federations, and support economic planning and development.

A third model is one that relies on bottom-up influence where the constituent units take initiative to shape policymaking across the federation. Characteristic of this model are strong horizontal councils, which constituent units use to gain leverage vis-à-vis the federal government and to engage in genuine horizontal coordination. Council outputs consist in joint statements addressed at the federal government or joint action of the constituent units. This model may also rely on strong informal contacts and be supported by intergovernmental relations divisions in core executives and line ministries. Given that the federal government does not participate in horizontal councils, it cannot dominate the intergovernmental agenda. This does not mean, however, that the federal government is not a relevant actor in intergovernmental relations.

The model most suitable for a given country depends on politics, context, and federal design. All three models are present one way or another in many federations and at different points in time, though one usually is the dominant one.

References

Auel, K. (2014). Intergovernmental relations in German federalism: Cooperative federalism, party politics and territorial conflicts. *Comparative European Politics*, *12*(4-5), 422-443.

Ayele, Z. A. & Fessha, Y. T. (2022). Intergovernmental relations and ethnic federalism in Ethiopia. In Y. T. Fessha, K. Kössler, & F. Palermo (Eds.), *Intergovernmental relations in divided societies* (pp. 113-132). London: Palgrave Macmillan.

Bednar, J. (2009). *The robust federation: Principles of design.* Cambridge: Cambridge University Press.

Behnke, N., & Mueller, S. (2017). The purpose of intergovernmental councils: A framework for analysis and comparison. *Regional & Federal Studies*, *27*(5), 507–527.

Boadway, R., & Shah, A. (2009). *Fiscal federalism: Principles and practice of multiorder governance*. Oxford: Oxford University Press.

Bolleyer, N. (2006). Federal dynamics in Canada, the United States, and Switzerland: How substates' internal organization affects intergovernmental relations. *Publius: The Journal of Federalism, 36*(4), 471–502.

Bolleyer, N. (2009). *Intergovernmental cooperation: Rational choices in federal systems and beyond*. Oxford: Oxford University Press.

Bolleyer, N. (2010). Why legislatures organise: Inter-parliamentary activism in federal systems and its consequences. *Journal of Legislative Studies, 16*(4), 411-437.

Bolleyer, N. (2011). The influence of political parties on policy coordination. *Governance: An International Journal of Policy, Administration and Institutions, 24*(3), 469-494.

Bolleyer, N., & Thorlakson, L. (2012). Beyond decentralization - The comparative study of interdependence in federal systems. *Publius: The Journal of Federalism, 42*(4), 566-591.

Braun, D., Ruiz-Palmero, C., & Schnabel, J. (2017). *Consolidation policies in federal states: Conflicts and solutions*. London: Routledge.

Cameron, D. (2001). The structures of intergovernmental relations. *International Social Science Journal, 167*, 121-127.

Cottarelli, C., & Guerguil, M. (2015). Introduction and overview. In C. Cottarelli, & M. Guerguil (Eds.), *Designing a European fiscal union: Lessons from the experience of fiscal federations* (pp. 1-13). London: Routledge.

Esselment, A. L. (2012). A little help from my friends: The partisan factor and intergovernmental negotiations in Canada. *Publius: The Journal of Federalism, 43*(4), 701-727.

Fenna, A. (2008). Commonwealth fiscal power and Australian federalism. *University of New South Wales Law Journal, 31*(2), 509-529.

Fenna, A. (2021). Australian federalism and the COVID-19 crisis. In R. Chattopadhyay et al. (Eds.), *Federalism and the response to COVID-19: A comparative analysis* (pp. 17-29). London: Routledge.

Fenna, A., & Schnabel, J. (2023). What is federalism? Some definitional clarification. *Publius: The Journal of Federalism*.

Fischer, M., Sciarini, P., & Traber, D. (2010). The silent reform of Swiss federalism: The new constitutional articles on education. *Swiss Political Science Review*, 16(4), 747-771.

Füglister, K., & Wasserfallen, F. (2014). Swiss federalism in a changing environment. *Comparative European Politics*, 12, 404-421.

Hegele, Y. (2018). Multidimensional interests in horizontal intergovernmental coordination: The case of the German Bundesrat. *Publius: The Journal of Federalism*, 48(2), 244-268.

Hegele, Y., & Behnke, N. (2017). Horizontal coordination in cooperative federalism: The purpose of ministerial conferences in Germany. *Regional & Federal Studies*, 27(5), 529-548.

Hueglin, T. O., & Fenna, A. (2015). *Comparative federalism: A systematic inquiry* (2nd ed.). Toronto: University of Toronto Press.

Jensen, M. D., Koop, C., & Tatham, M. (2014). Coping with power dispersion? Autonomy, coordination and control in multilevel systems. *Journal of European Public Policy*, 21(nov.), 1237-1254.

Leon, S. (2017). Intergovernmental councils in Spain: Challenges and opportunities in a changing political context. *Regional & Federal Studies*, 27(5), 645-665.

Mendoza Ruiz, J., & Grin, E. J. (Eds.). (2020). *Federaciones de las Américas: Descentralización, relaciones intergubernamentales y recentralización*. Instituto Nacional de Administración Pública, A.C.

Mueller, S., & Fenna, A. (2022). Dual versus administrative federalism: Origins and evolution of two models. *Publius: The Journal of Federalism*, 52(4), 525-552.

Nugent, J. (2009). *Safeguarding federalism: How states protect their interests in national policymaking*. Norman: University of Oklahoma Press.

Oates, W. E. (1999). An essay on fiscal federalism. *Journal of Economic Literature*, 37(3), 1120-1149.

OECD. (2020). *The territorial impact of COVID-19: Managing the crisis across levels of government*. Geneve: OECD Publishing.

Osaghae, E. E. (2015). Nigeria: Struggling to formalize and decentralize intergovernmental relations. In J. Poirier, C. Saunders, & J. Kincaid (Eds.), *Intergovernmental* relations in federal systems: Comparative structures and dynamics (pp. 272-304). Oxford: Oxford University Press.

Painter, M. (2001). Multi-level governance and the emergence of collaborative federal institutions in Australia. *Policy & Politics, 29*(2), 137-150.

Papillon, M., & Simeon, R. (2004). The weakest link? First Ministers' conferences in Canadian intergovernmental relations. In J. P. Meekinson, H. Telford, & H. Lazar (Eds.), *Canada: The state of the federation 2002. Reconsidering the institutions of Canadian federalism* (pp. 113-140). Montreal: McGill-Queen's University Press.

Phillimore, J., & Fenna, A. (2017). Intergovernmental councils and centralization in Australian federalism. *Regional & Federal Studies, 27*(5), 597-621.

Poirier, J., & Saunders, C. (2015a). Comparing intergovernmental relations in federal systems: An introduction. In J. Poirier, C. Saunders, & J. Kincaid (Eds.), *Intergovernmental relations in federal systems: Comparative structures and dynamics* (pp. 1-13). Oxford: Oxford University Press.

Poirier, J., & Saunders, C. (2015b). Conclusion: Comparative experiences of intergovernmental relations in federal systems. In J. Poirier, C. Saunders, & J. Kincaid (Eds.), *Intergovernmental relations in federal systems: Comparative structures and dynamics* (pp. 440-498). Oxford: Oxford University Press.

Poirier, J., Saunders, C., & Kincaid, J. (Eds.). (2015). *Intergovernmental relations in federal systems: Comparative structures and dynamics*. Oxford: Oxford University Press.

Popelier, P. (2021). What is federalism? In search of building blocks for a new federal theory. In *Dynamic Federalism: A New Theory for Cohesion and Regional Autonomy* (1st ed.). London: Routledge.

Scharpf, F. W. (1988). The joint-decision trap: Lessons from German federalism and European integration. *Public Administration, 66*, 239-278.

Scharpf, F. W. (1994). Games real actors could play. *Journal of Theoretical Politics, 6*(1), 27-53.

Scharpf, F. W. (1997). *Games real actors play: Actor-centered institutionalism in policy research*. Oxford: Oxford University Press.

Scharpf, F. W. (2008). Community, diversity and autonomy: The challenges of reforming German federalism. *German Politics, 17*(4), 509-521.

Schnabel, J. (2020). *Managing interdependencies in federal systems: Intergovernmental councils and the making of public policy*. London: Palgrave Macmillan.

Schnabel, J., Freiburghaus, R., & Hegele, Y. (2022). Crisis management in federal states: The role of peak intergovernmental councils in Germany and Switzerland during the COVID-19 pandemic. *DMS - der moderne staat, 15*(1), 42-61.

Schnabel, J., & Mueller, S. (2017). Vertical influence or horizontal coordination? The purpose of intergovernmental councils in Switzerland. *Regional & Federal Studies, 27*(5), 549-572.

Simmons, J. M. (2004). Securing the threads of cooperation in the tapestry of intergovernmental relations: Does the institutionalization of ministerial conferences matter? In J. P. Meekinson, H. Telford, & H. Lazar (Eds.), *Canada: The state of the federation 2002. Reconsidering the institutions of Canadian federalism* (pp. 285-311). Montreal: McGill-Queen's University Press.

Simmons, J. M. (2017). Canadian multilateral intergovernmental institutions and the limits of institutional innovation. *Regional & Federal* Studies, *27*(5), 573-596.

Trench, A. (2006). Intergovernmental relations: In search of a theory. In S. L. Greer (Ed.), *Territory, democracy and justice: Regionalism and federalism in western democracies* (pp. 224-256). London: Palgrave Macmillan.

Watts, R. L. (1999). *The spending power in federal systems: A comparative study. Institute of Intergovernmental Relations*, Kingston: Queen's University.

13

MANAGING INTERGOVERNMENTAL RELATIONS IN BRAZIL: TYPES, STRUCTURES, AND FUNCTIONING

Eduardo Grin

Introduction

Describing and analyzing the models, designs and functioning of intergovernmental relations (IGR) between spheres of government in Brazil since 1988 is the focus of this chapter. However, we must first consider the general characteristics of Brazilian federalism [see chapter by Marta Arretche in this volume]. Federal systems may or may not create mechanisms for IGRs. In general, negotiations between different governments are necessary for policy coordination (Hueglin & Fenna, 2015; Watts, 2008). The more formal IGR forums are, the stronger the coordination between different governments (Bolleyer, 2006; Schnabel, 2020). These forums function as channels to bring federal and subnational governments closer to working together based on "the incorporation of interests and preferences, as well as expertise, of the constituent units in their decision-making" (Fenna & Schnabel, 2023, p. 9).

Considering that, the chapter approaches Brazilian IGR and its four institutionalized types of intergovernmental relations:

- Forum made up of generalists and of a vertical nature (Federative Articulation Committee).
- Forums formed by generalists of a horizontal nature (Forum of Governors and Interstate Consortia).
- Forums formed by sectoral and vertical specialists (intergovernmental councils in the areas of health, social assistance, finance and education).

- Forums formed by sectoral and horizontal specialists (health, social assistance, finance, and education) at the state and municipal level and inter-municipal consortia.

For Wright (1988), political-administrative generalists are usually elected political leaders who are responsible for all government actions while specialists are the leaders and administrators responsible for public policy sectors. Vertical arenas are made up of more than one level of government while horizontal arenas are made up of governments of the same level.

The main argument of this chapter is that neither the concentration of power in the hands of the federal government nor the decentralization of responsibilities to states and municipalities has been able to address the increasing complexities of IGR in Brazilian federation since 1988. Because of this, the emergence of different IGR arrangements has been an attempt to face challenges in the functioning of the federation. Vertical and horizontal cooperation channels discussions about common problems into formal arenas, although not always successfully.

Formal mechanisms of IGR in Brazilian Federation

The Committee of Federative Articulation: generalist and vertical cooperation model

A forum of vertical intergovernmental relations based on jurisdictional lines was installed after 2003. The federal government created an original forum, considering the comparative experience, called Committee on Federative Articulation (CFA), formed by national and municipal representatives. In other countries where this type of forum exists, state governments play a prominent role. The CFA was created in the first Lula administration (2003-2006) to facilitate a federative "meeting of agendas" between the central government and the national municipal associations. With the CFA, the federative pact acquired political relevance by being housed as an advisory body of the Secretariat for Institutional Relations (SRI) of the Presidency of the Republic, with the committee acting as a direct representative of the head of government. However, when compared with the German and Australian experiences, where premiers oversee cooperation arenas, the CFA did not have the same political and constitutional density (Grin & Abrucio, 2018a; 2018b). The CFA was established by presidential decree, a notable difference from cases such as Germany,

Switzerland, South Africa, Canada and Australia, as its constitutional and/or legal support provided a weaker intergovernmental decision-making authority (Grin, 2020). Thus, this forum essentially acted as an articulation and coordination structure, lacking command or enforcement power over other federal bodies. Efforts to promote "intergovernmental partnership" focused on "jurisdictions" (territories) did not overcome the challenges of involving "functions" (sectoral policies) in the proposed initiatives (Grin & Abrucio, 2018).

Another challenge for CFA to build its federative agenda was to overcome the "joint decision trap", as its deliberations were adopted only by consensus. However, unlike the German and Australian cases, its decisions had no guarantee that they would be implemented, as this was a forum for advice and consultation without the power to adopt binding agendas. The fact that themes of municipal interest did not generate agreement between the federal bodies that composed it exemplifies this "trap": by not being approved by consensus, its practical effect was to maintain the status quo of actions implemented by existing sectoral bodies at the federal level (Grin & Abrucio, 2018). Compared to the experience of the German, Canadian and Australian territorial cooperation forums, this was the main reason for CFA's failure. This issue can differentiate forums with enforcement capacity from those that are nothing more than "pseudo-arenas" (Pressman, 1975) or "advisory groups" (Inwood, Johns, & O'Reilly, 2011).

In summary, given the international experience – and given the importance of this type of forum having to hold intragovernmental power to influence issues of federative inequality that affect municipal administration – institutions such as CFA have limited power resources to act in the intergovernmental arena. Because of that, after an initial success with pressing federative demands, the CFA lost political force and momentum after 2011.

A new design of the Federation Council was initiated by the current Lula government, starting in January 2023, and now considers the participation of states (represented by the Forum of Governors and interstate consortia), as well as associations of municipalities. Considering the international experience, this seems to be a promising path, opening up a new research agenda on IGRs in Brazil and from a comparative perspective. For example, the inclusion of interstate consortia in the future Federal Council is a novelty in comparative literature. However, as the Federation Council was recently established, it is not yet possible to assess its results and functioning.

Governors' Forum and the experiences of Interstate Consortia

Regarding horizontal intergovernmental relations based on jurisdictional lines, The Governors Forum (FG) was established in 2017 and officially called the Permanent Forum of Governors of the States and the Federal District. This forum acts as an informal entity for articulating positions that brings together the 27 state governments represented by their governors. Four factors have driven the FG:

- Fiscal nature: the loss of relevance of states in Brazilian federalism and the burden of maintaining the provision of public policies.
- Health emergency: role assumed in the COVID-19 pandemic with the absence of the federal government.
- Institutional learning: the previous experience of the forums of governors in the regions of the country that could be extended to the national arena as a way of reinforcing the intergovernmental lobby with the federal government in matters of tax nature, federal transfers and the federative pact itself regarding the constitutionally guaranteed state autonomy.
- Federative disputes: the role played by the Bolsonaro government and its vision of a confrontational federalism with subnational entities (Abrucio et al., 2020).

The crisis triggered by COVID-19 unexpectedly intensified the cooperation and coordination of common public policies among governors, as well as the protection of their autonomy. This trend had already been underway due to the lack of political authority and the federative conflict initiated by President Bolsonaro. It remains to be seen whether the states will continue to advance in their collective action agenda. However, considering the Forum's influence on the federal government since 2020, particularly in its recent efforts to renegotiate tax and fiscal issues with the newly sworn-in Lula government, the likelihood of it strengthening as an arena of intergovernmental cooperation in the coming years has potential to increase.

Another form of horizontal cooperation between generalists is the recent experience of interstate consortia. Also, the existent literature is still incipient, but some works have been analyzing this intergovernmental cooperation arrangement (Brom, 2021). There are currently four interstate consortia legally supported by the federal law that, since 2005, govern the creation and operation of public consortia (South and Southeast Integration Consortium (COSUD), Interstate Consortium for the Development of Central Brazil (BrC), Interstate Consortium for Sustainable Development of the Legal Amazon, and the so-called Consortium of the Northeast. The most consolidated model is the Consortium of the Northeast, which brings together all nine states and was created in 2019, also in response to the intergovernmental relationship crisis generated by the Bolsonaro government.

By expanding the horizontal cooperation arenas and reinforcing collective action among state governments, Brazilian federalism aligns more closely with other countries where this has been a longstanding reality. For example, in Germany, regional forums formed by the Landers function (Lottha & Blumenthal, 2015; Schnabel, 2020), while in Canada, the Council of Federation brings together provincial premiers (Adams, Bergeron, & Bonnard, 2015). Similarly, in the United States, we see the Council of State Governments and the National Association of Governors (Bowman, 2017), and in Mexico, the National Conference of Governors (Ruiz, 2020). The novelty in the Brazilian case, from a comparative perspective, lies in the interstate consortia established as legal entities in accordance with the federal legislation governing these arrangements.

Sectoral and vertical cooperation in Brazilian federalism

As for vertical intergovernmental relations based on sectoral lines, Brazilian federalism intensified the decentralization of social policies to states and municipalities after 1988, which soon gave rise to the need for federative coordination. This demand was initially more pronounced in the areas of health and later in social assistance policy, as both are organized into a single national system requiring formal agreement on financing and operational rules among the three spheres of government. In the case of education, due to the previous trajectory of greater autonomy of state and municipal school networks, this format of intergovernmental cooperation is more fragile, limited in scope, and organized on a more informal basis. In the field of fiscal federalism, the National Council for Fiscal Policy (CONFAZ) has been operating since 1975 and had its existence ratified by the Federal Constitution (FC). These are the most relevant sectoral and vertical intergovernmental forums in the experience of Brazilian federalism, and their main purposes are coordination and information exchange.

The dominant paradigm is the Unified Health System (SUS) that, since 1993, institutionalized a collegiate and consensual federative coordination and decision-making style (Grin, Lotta, & Abrucio, 2023). As an attribution shared by all the states in the Brazilian federation, the challenge lies in defining deliberative and decision-making mechanisms. This challenge has been addressed with the creation of institutional decision-making forums in which municipal, state, and federal managers participate. The Tripartite Interagency Committee (CIT) brings together officials from the three levels of government, while in Brazil's 27 states Bipartite Interagency Committees (CIBs) bring together state and municipal officials (Leandro & Meniccuci, 2018).

Brazil has made significant strides in vertical sectoral cooperation since 1988, particularly in health and social assistance which are organized under the institutional design of a unified national system of public policy. These arrangements act as federative safeguards which was fundamental to avoid encroaching actions by the federal government (Bednar, 2009), especially in the health sector during the COVID-19 pandemic through tripartite cooperation.

In this model, the federal government is responsible for coordination, regulation, financing, and wielding its "power of the purse". States and municipalities are relevant actors that participate in the federative cooperation arrangement but are dependent on federal transfers. In addition, many states and municipalities have less qualified bureaucracies, which results in a more asymmetrical relationship with the federal government regarding decisions impacting subnational management. Therefore, despite the progress in federative cooperation, the model resembles the Australian experience more closely than the German and Swiss cases, where the institutionality of cooperation is more independent of the national government's actions.

However, the systems model has made a significant contribution to Brazilian federalism, with other areas attempting to follow suit, although without the same success. This is evident in various sectors such as public safety, environmental conservation, sports, traffic, social interest housing, culture, housing, drug policy, and the promotion of racial equality (Grin &

Abrucio, 2021). Due to its relevance, it is worth noting the creation in 2009, but not its implementation, of the National Education System (Abrucio, 2010). Less successful has been the trajectory of intergovernmental cooperation in fiscal federalism as race to the bottom processes have produced more competition between states as well as between municipalities than federative pacts. This continues to be an Achilles heel of Brazilian fiscal federalism, especially in a post-COVID-19 pandemic context in which states and municipalities have lost a lot of revenue.

Sectoral and horizontal cooperation in Brazilian federalism

Considering the horizontal intergovernmental relations based on sectoral lines, the experiences of Brazilian federalism in this IGR format can be organized as follows: a) 29 state and municipal public policy councils that bring together managers from each area to agree on decisions aimed at influencing the federative debate at the national level or organizing the implementation of the policy in states or municipalities; b) 488 inter-municipal consortia, which in Brazil are predominantly organized on a sectoral and non-jurisdictional basis. The so-called multipurpose consortium is formed by the local governments as jurisdictions because it is organized along territorial lines. This type of consortium is far from being the norm, to the extent that it is not known how many exist in the country. The main purposes of these forums are to influence public policies, especially at the federal level, and to facilitate coordination and information exchange.

These councils have influenced federal decisions in different ways in each policy. As a rule, the federal government does not formulate policies without formally or informally consulting these bodies. Many councils are not dependent on the political will of the national government, and they can work more autonomously because their members are only states or municipalities. Subnational units can, based on their constitutional autonomy, choose to establish this type of forum without requiring federal approval.

The second format for IGRs of this type are inter-municipal consortia. Consortia have existed in Brazil since the 1960s, but there was a significant growth after the Consortia Law established the possibility of creating public consortia. The new legal rules represent an advancement generated by FC, which redefined the notion of public services by stating that they can be collectively provided by two or more federal units, including national and state spheres. The Public Consortia Law consolidated the legal bases of this type of federative cooperation among municipalities.

Consortia can be configured as public law associations ratified by law by the municipal Executive and Legislative powers of all participant municipalities. Public consortia consist of federative articulation structures that enable intergovernmental cooperation actions and shared management of public responsibilities, strengthening the administration of local governments. In other words, public consortia are simply groups of governments that come together to jointly provide a certain service. Despite heterogeneous advance in territorial terms and by public policies, the inductions generated by the new legislation continue to impact the decisions of municipalities in favor of consortia. By creating more regularity and predictability in intermunicipal associations, legislation assumed a key role as an explanatory variable (Grin, 2021). According to the Consortium Observatory of the National Confederation of Municipalities, in 2019, 4,074 municipalities were associated in Brazil under the public consortium modality (73% of the 5,570 Brazilian municipalities). If consortia are formed to generate economies of scale and organizational gains, the numbers of this phenomenon in Brazil serve as a good initial indication and promising evidence (Grin, 2021).

In the two forms of sectoral horizontal cooperation there are differences in terms of the results generated for the subnational public administration. Councils and forums serve as arenas for articulation, agreement and dissemination of information, in addition to influencing the formulation of public policies. On the other hand, intermunicipal consortia primarily impact the implementation of public policies, as they aim to compensate for the administrative, technical and financial deficiencies of municipalities through instruments of economy of scale.

Conclusion

Brazilian federalism contains a paradox that could pose challenges for the implementation of IGR arrangements. On the one hand, the national government wields significant constitutional, regulatory, and financial power that affect constituent units. On the other hand, the decentralization that reinforced the autonomy of states and municipalities has led to a centrifugal process and difficult intergovernmental cooperation. Both aspects would be hallmarks of Brazilian federalism after 1988, although there are constitutional devices that emphasize the existence of common responsibilities between the three spheres of government and that refer to the need for intergovernmental cooperation. This chapter showed four different paths for building cooperative arrangements of IGR in Brazilian federalism. By different routes, IGRs are an inescapable reality of the Brazilian federation. However, if there have been advances in the format of IGRs, there are gaps and open questions for further research on the subject.

The experience of the CFA, a unique case in comparative federalism of vertical cooperation on jurisdictional bases because it does not include the States, shows that the format was not entirely successful in establishing a federative arena. The new design of a Federation Council was defined by the current Lula government in January 2023, right at the beginning of its mandate, which highlights the relevance of this issue for the government. The Council of Federation incorporated the States (represented by the Forum of Governors and interstate consortia), as well as associations of municipalities.

Horizontal cooperation on jurisdictional bases is relatively recent (the FG has existed for less than six years, and interstate consortia only began to be implemented in 2015). There is a need to deepen academic investigation into this emerging trajectory of IGR in Brazilian federalism. In Brazil, the research agenda on the role of states in the federation has only recently gained traction after almost three decades of prioritizing studies on the role of municipalities.

In vertical and sectoral cooperation, there are three relevant issues. First, in health and social assistance, the CIT and the CIBs are managerial committees and not intergovernmental councils according to the literature (Schnabel, 2020). Second, we need a better understanding of why the mimicry of national policy systems was unsuccessful in other public policies, which also affects the functioning of public administration. Thirdly, it is necessary to deepen the research agenda, in the field of fiscal federalism, of the role of CONFAZ in the face of the persistence of the fiscal war and the unilateralism of the states in the taxation policies that generates race-to-the-bottom problems. This issue looms large on the federative agenda, especially considering the approval of a tax reform that will begin implementation in 2027 and will entail many changes in the current design of fiscal federalism.

In sectoral horizontal cooperation, intermunicipal consortia are well established and generate direct effects for public administration. The results in economy of scale and scope, dissemination of good practices, expansion in the provision of services and territorial planning are robust. However, little is known about the outcomes generated for local populations and how municipalities use consortia to qualify their management in the sectors in which they form a consortium. This is a welcome research agenda.

In a federation as unequal and asymmetric as Brazil, several RIG routes are expected to promote closer collaboration between the three levels of government seeking to improve public administration. The existence of four institutional designs of IGRs demonstrates that intergovernmental cooperation has served as a vital tool in service delivery and policymaking.

References

Abrucio, F. A. et al. (2020). Combating COVID-19 under Bolsonaro's federalism: a case of intergovernmental incoordination. *Revista de Administração Pública*, *54*(4), 663-677.

Abrucio, F. L. (2010). A dinâmica federativa da educação brasileira: diagnóstico e propostas de aperfeiçoamento. In R. P. O Oliveira, & W. Santana (Eds.), *Educação e federalismo no Brasil: combater as desigualdades, garantir a diversidade* (pp. 39-70). Genebra: UNESCO.

Adam, M.A., Bergeron, J. & Bonnard, M. (2015). Intergovernmental Relations in Canada: competing visions and diverse dynamics. In J. Poirier, C. Saunders, & J. Kincaid (Eds.), *Intergovernmental Relations in Federal Systems: comparative structures and dynamics* (pp. 135-173). Oxford: Oxford University Press.

Bednar, J. (2009). *The robust federation: Principles of design*. Cambridge University Press. Retrieved from https://doi:10.1017/S0022381609991009

Bolleyer, N. (2006). Federal Dynamics in Canada, the United States, and Switzerland: How Substates' Internal Organization Affects Intergovernmental Relations. *Publius: The Journal of Federalism*, *36*(4), 471-502.

Bowman, A. O. (2017). Intergovernmental councils in United States. *Regional and Federal Studies*, *27*(5), 623-643.

Brom, G. P. (2021). *Cooperação federativa interestadual no brasil: o caso do consórcio do Nordeste*. São Paulo: Escola de Administração de Empresas de São Paulo.

Confederação Nacional dos Municípios (2020). *Observatório dos Consórcios*. Retrieved March 25, 2024, from https://consorcios.cnm.org.br/

Fenna, A., & Schnabel, J. (2023). What is Federalism? Some Definitional Clarification. *Publius: The Journal of Federalism, 54*(2), 179-200.

Grin, E. J., & Abrucio, F. L. (2021). Hybridism as a national policy style: paths and dilemmas of the majoritarian and consensus approaches in Brazil. *Revista Brasileira de Ciência Política, 35*, 1-59.

Grin, E. J., Lotta, G. S., & Abrucio, F. L. (2023). Intergovernmental relations and public administration: the cases of public health, education, and social assistance policies in Brazil. In F. M. Navarro, & J. D. P Guadarrama. *Los nuevos desafíos de la administración pública en una esperada época de postpandemia* (pp. 261-286). Tirant Lo Blanch.

Grin, E. J. (2021). Capacidades políticas locais e a realidade dos consórcios intermunicipais na federação brasileira. In E. J. Grin, D. J. Demarco, & F. L. Abrucio (Eds.), *Capacidades estatais municipais: o universo desconhecido no federalismo brasileiro* (pp. 317-35). Porto Alegre: Editora da UFRGS/CEGOV.

Grin, E. J. (2020). Arranjos federativos de cooperação territorial e o caso Comitê de Articulação Federativa no Brasil: quando poder de enforcement e de suporte jurídico importam. In L. S. B. Almeida, M. I. A. Rodrigues, R. M. C. Silveira, & C. M. O. Melo (Eds.), *Contribuições do Campo de Públicas: um olhar sobre a democracia no século XXI e os desafios para a gestão pública* (pp. 44-76). Belo Horizonte: Fundação João Pinheiro.

Grin, E. J., & Abrucio, F. L (2018). O Comitê de Articulação Federativa no governo Lula: os percalços da cooperação territorial. *Revista Brasileira de Ciências Sociais, 33*(7), 1-24.

Hueglin, T. O., & A. Fenna (2015). *Comparative Federalism: A Systematic Inquiry* (2nd ed.). Toronto: University of Toronto Press.

Inwoods, G. J., Johns, C. M., & O'Reily P. (2011). *Intergovernmental policy capacity in Canada. Inside the worlds of finance, environment, trade, and health.* Montreal: McGill-Queens's University Press.

Leandro, J. G., & Menicucci, T. M. G. (2018). Governança federativa nas políticas de saúde e assistência social: processo decisório nas Comissões Intergestores Tripartite (2009-2012). *Revista do Serviço Público, 69*(4), 817-848.

Lopreato, F. L. C. (2022). Federalismo brasileiro: origem, evolução e desafios. *Economia e Sociedade, 31*(1), 1-41.

Lotha, R., & Blumenthal, J. (2015). Intergovernmental Relations in the Federal Republic of Germany: complex co-operation and party politics. In J. Poirier, C. Saunders, & J. Kincaid (Eds.), *Intergovernmental Relations in Federal Systems: comparative structures and dynamics* (pp. 206-238). Oxford: Oxford University Press.

Pressman, J. L. (1975). *Federal programs and city politics*. Berkeley: University of California Press.

Ruiz, J. M. (2020). El desequilibrio entre las salvaguardas federales y la inercia de jerarquíaen México. In J. M. Ruiz, & E. J. Grin. (Eds.). *Federaciones de las Américas: descentralización, relaciones intergubernamentales y recentralización* (pp. 295-378). INAP.

Schnabel, J. (2020). *Managing Interdependencies in Federal Systems: Intergovernmental Councils and the Making of Public Policy*. London: Pallgrave Mcmillan.

Watts, R. L. (2008). *Comparing federal systems* (3rd ed.). Institute of Intergovernmental Relations.

Wright, D. S. (1988). *Understanding intergovernmental relations*. Brooks: Cole Publishing Company.

14

NEW PATHS FOR BRAZILIAN FEDERALISM: THE CREATION OF THE COUNCIL OF THE FEDERATION

André Luis Nogueira da Silva
Elaine Cristina Lício

Introduction

During a meeting with governors and mayors addressing the issue of school violence in April 2023, President Lula made the following statement: "I don't have a solution for the case, and I want to share your wisdom, a little wisdom from each one, to allow us to build a definitive solution". The speech demonstrates a willingness for dialogue and the collective construction of national public policies. It also represents a movement to rebuild a cooperative federative culture, a perspective that had been solidified in Brazil since the 1988 Constitution (Franzese, 2010; Arretche, 2012) and had been severely undermined during the Bolsonaro Government (2019-2021).

The current context of democratic reconstruction, therefore, involves a return to cooperative logic in federative relations. This perspective is manifested not only by resuming dialogue with states and municipalities in different public policy sectors but also by the institutional innovation of creating the Council of the Federation.

The establishment of a federative dialogue space composed of political leaders from executive powers responds to attacks on democracy and the conflict-ridden logic that marked the previous government (Abrucio et al., 2020). This space can also deepen the culture of federative cooperation in the management of public policies in the country. Moreover, it addresses challenges already present in the Brazilian Federation, which is tripartite but lacked a negotiating table with such a composition.

This text aims to present the Council of the Federation – an institution created by presidential decree in April 2023 –, its motivations for creation, potentials, and challenges. The proposal is to reconstruct the political-institutional context that allowed its origin, characterize its institutional design, and outline the role it can play in shaping new cooperative dynamics for Brazilian federalism.

In addition to this introduction, this chapter has three more parts. In the next one, we characterize the political-institutional context of the Brazilian federation, emphasizing its institutional design outlined by the current Constitution and highlighting the trajectory of deepening intergovernmental cooperation that was interrupted in 2019. We also point out how the cooperative crisis in the Brazilian federation created conditions, as a kind of side effect, for the creation of the Council of the Federation. Next, we describe the characteristics of the Council of the Federation and how it intends to operate and promote the improvement of Brazilian federalism. Finally, we offer brief considerations on the challenges to be overcome for this new institution to gain legitimacy and serve as a tool for improving public policies and consolidating the Brazilian Welfare State.

Political-Institutional Context of the Brazilian Federation Post-1988

In Brazil, historically, the perspective of a federal state has been linked to democratic ideals (Silva et al., 2023). This was evident in the first Republican Constitution of 1891, which transformed its former provinces into the "United States of Brazil" in its first article, giving them powers, at least formal, over the national decision-making process. The explicit mimicry of the North American institutional configuration was limited to the normative design, as, in Brazil, the context of regional disputes did not lead to major armed uprisings. In other words, political negotiations did not face significant barriers, with the people almost "bestialized" witnessing the monarchy's downfall (Carvalho, 1987).

The other democratic constitutional experiments that Brazil underwent later – in 1946 and in 1988, which is still in effect today – aimed to overcome authoritarian governments and had the restoration of political power to governors as one of their main pillars. This was because previous authoritarian regimes (1937 and 1964) had curtailed the political autonomy of the states.

The 1988 Constitution went further. It not only restored the powers of the states but also granted municipalities the status of a federative entity. The Brazilian federation, therefore, came to include three levels of government with political, administrative, and fiscal autonomy. Additionally, the parliament is bicameral [see also chapter by Cláudio Couto in this volume], with representation of states in the Federal Senate (elected by the majoritarian system) and representation of the population in the Chamber of Deputies (elected by the proportional system with the state as the district). Furthermore, there is a Federal Supreme Court with the authority to settle federative conflicts.

The Brazilian federative design becomes complex with the perspective that municipalities are not subordinates to the states and the absence of territorial representation in both national and state parliaments. Therefore, the inclusion of municipal interests in national and state decision-making processes requires other channels of dialogue to occur (Silva, 2020).

Nevertheless, the constitutional framework aimed to deepen federative cooperation by stipulating a wide range of shared responsibilities for the three levels of government. These include health, education, science and technology, environment, culture, poverty reduction, etc. In a country with profound socioeconomic and regional inequalities, federative coordination and cooperation are crucial for its development.

In the early 1990s, the federal government began developing national policies and sectoral governance structures at varying paces and different formats, some of which were established under the label of "national public policy systems" (Unified Health System, National Environmental System, National Culture System, National Education System) (Silva et al., 2023a). Although autonomous, the adherence of states and municipalities to these systems or even national programs requires an inductive role from the central government. In addition to financial incentives, the federal government also created sectoral federative negotiation spaces to serve as instruments for managing these systems or national policies and the consequent expansion of public services, especially in the social welfare policies (Arretche, 1999; Abrucio, 2005).

This is the case with the Unified Health System, envisaged by the 1988 Constitution and regulated in 1990. The creation of the Tripartite Intermanager Commission (CIT) in 1993 aimed to bring representatives of federal, state, and municipal managers to the same negotiation table to decide on the operationalization of national health policies. At that time, the sectorial federalism cooperation was flourishing in Brazil. The federative dialogue and deliberation channel that had been created not only expanded cooperative practices but also fostered a new ideology about the importance of intergovernmental cooperation for the successful implementation of health policies.

Despite the success in the health sector, the formulation and implementation processes of other sectoral policies did not progress at the same pace. In many cases, cooperative governance structures did not function well, with a low degree of institutionalization or lacking legitimacy within the policy community. Sectoral specificities are so present in the grammar of public policies in Brazil that it is possible to observe the incidence of a multiplicity of "federative pacts." Moreover, even within the governance of the Unified Health System, some decisions go beyond the sectoral perspective, requiring decisions to be made at the level of the political leaders of the federative units, as is already the case in other federations such as Canada, Germany, and Australia.

Some studies highlight the importance of collaborative political leadership for the promotion and success of intergovernmental policies and programs (Agranoff, 2012). From the perspective of intergovernmental coordination, Schnabel (2020) emphasizes that intergovernmental councils can ensure that national political decisions are made in a reliable environment with respect for the autonomy of federative entities, functioning as federative safeguards [see also chapter by Johanna Schnabel in this volume]. A new institution, created in 2005 during the first Lula administration, sought to address this institutional gap.

The Federative Articulation Committee (CAF) brought together representatives from the federal government and municipal entities to discuss, deliberate, and formulate policies to strengthen the federation. However, it lacked decision-making authority and intra-governmental enforcement resources (Grin, 2018). During that period, states were not part of the negotiation table, possibly due to a lack of horizontal cohesion, a failure to recognize the importance of states for the universalization of social policies (the federal government's primary agenda), or even a political choice to distance from state oligarchies (Borges, 2007).

Alternating between periods of greater or lesser activity, the Federative Articulation Committee existed until 2019 when, early in the Bolsonaro government, a decree extinguished it along with hundreds of social participation councils and committees. This was one of the first moves of that government to reduce or even extinguish dialogue with federative entities.

In addition to dismantling participatory structures, the Bolsonaro Government (2019-2022) also worked to dismantle numerous national public policies that had undergone a process of institutionalization and learning since the 1988 Constitution. The demobilization of state capacities in various sectors and the dismantling of public policies were actions that characterized the entire Bolsonaro administration (Gomide et al., 2023). Obviously, such dismantling affected the operation of the Brazilian federation, leading to the interruption of programs and public services, as seen in the case of social assistance (Paiva, 2023).

The lack of dialogue was accompanied by a conflict-ridden dynamic in relations with states and municipalities, as well as a weakening of the coordinating role of the federal government in implementing public policies (Abrucio et al., 2020). The federative conflict became more pronounced and explicit during the pandemic. At that time, the federal government began questioning the epidemiological records made by states and municipalities, as well as acting to delegitimize the Tripartite Intermanagers Commission of the Unified Health System (Palotti et al., 2023). The Bolsonaro government even filed a lawsuit in the Federal Supreme Court challenging subnational autonomy in combating the pandemic – a move rejected by the court ministers.

As a result of the conflict-ridden context, there was a horizontal alignment among federative entities. In the case of Health, the National Council of State Health Secretaries attempted, in the absence of the federal government, to promote some form of federative coordination. The Northeast Consortium, which brings together all states in the region, also began coordinating the actions of its members. This movement also revitalized the functioning of other existing interstate consortia, such as the Central Brazil and Legal Amazon consortia. Throughout 2019, governors in the South and Southeast regions announced their intention to formalize the South-Southeast Integration Consortium, although the process has not yet concluded [see also chapter by Eduardo Grin in this volume]. The absence of federative coordination by the central government during the pandemic also prompted states to collaborate more closely with their municipalities, extending federative coordination to the subnational level even in states with little tradition in this type of action (Gomes et al., 2022).

The results of the 2022 elections brought a new vitality to the democratic regime and cooperative Brazilian federalism. However, shortly after the new president took office, the world witnessed an attack by Bolsonaro's supporters on the headquarters of the three branches of the Republic. In a political-institutional response to the anti-democratic attack, the 27 governors joined the President and signed a letter, known as the "Brasília Letter", in support of democracy and the strengthening of public consortia as instruments of federative cooperation, and agreed to establish the Council of the Federation.

Institutional Design of the Council of the Federation

The decree creating the Council of the Federation was published on April 18, 2023. The Council was conceived as an integrating body and promoter of cooperation among federative entities, serving as a space for negotiation, coordination, and agreement on common priority strategies and actions. Decisions of the Council of the Federation will be made through consensus and should aim at sustainable economic development and the reduction of social and regional inequalities.

The decisions of the Council are not binding but will serve as a guide for the actions of the various levels of government in promoting public policies and institutional reforms. Respecting the autonomy of federative entities, acting within the constitutional competencies of the executive powers, improving federative cooperation instruments, integrating with other sectoral instruments, and building political commitments are the guidelines that underpin the role of the Council of the Federation. Its objectives include agreeing on a common federation priority agenda, contributing to the formulation of national policies and the development of institutional reforms, strengthening federative cooperation and coordination, conducting studies to support evidence-based decision-making, and promoting the dissemination of successful policies. In general, the Council aims to enhance and strengthen Brazilian executive federalism as it establishes a forum with representation from political leaders at various levels of government.

It consists of 18 members, with guaranteed parity among the three levels of government. Chaired by the President, the federal government is also represented by the Vice President, Minister of Institutional Relations,

Minister of the Civil House, and two ministers chosen according to the meeting's agenda. In the case of state governments, the representation includes a governor indicated by the National Governors' Forum, one by the Northeast Consortium, one by the Legal Amazon Consortium, and one by the Central Brazil Consortium. The South-Southeast Integration Consortium indicates two governors, one for each region. Finally, municipal entities indicate two representatives each: the National Front of Mayors, the National Confederation of Municipalities, and the Brazilian Municipalities Association. It is essential to note that municipal entities had already participated in the Federative Articulation Committee (CAF) experience and have different types of representation.

The governance structure of the Council includes, in addition to the plenary, an executive secretariat, in charge of the Special Secretariat for Federative Affairs of the Ministry of Institutional Relations, and a Technical Secretariat, which also has parity composition indicated by the same actors who make up the Council's Plenary.

The Technical Secretariat is akin to heart of the Council. Its role involves processing the agendas to be addressed in the Technical Chambers and collaboratively constructing the political commitments with the councilors before deliberation in the Plenary. The members of subnational governments typically hold leadership positions within consortia and entities. Therefore, they play central roles in the political negotiation process and in bridging the gap between technical elements (evidence) and political considerations in decision-making.

The first Plenary meeting took place on October 25th, 2023, at the *Palácio do Planalto* (federal executive power headquarters). The councilors decided to create three Technical Chambers: Strengthening Management and Federative Cooperation, Sustainable Economic Development and Climate Change, and Social Policies and Combating Inequalities. In November of the same year, the first meeting of the Technical Secretariat was held, which agreed on the priorities of each Chamber, operating dynamics, and work plan.

With the start of its operation, this new institution inaugurates a new way of operating the Brazilian federation, being able to produce learning and changes in the country's federative culture. The following years are therefore full of challenges for the Council of the Federation, which, if overcome, can make important contributions to Brazilian federalism.

Final Considerations: The Challenge of Building a New Federative Political Culture

The Council of the Federation emerges at a time of rehabilitation of democratic institutions and of the rebuilding of trust between federative entities. It goes beyond merely proposing to fill an institutional void that already existed prior to the cooperative erosion caused by the Bolsonaro Government. The establishment of a tripartite table, chaired by the President and comprising representatives of political leaders from states and municipalities across the country, has the potential to inaugurate a new way of conceptualizing the federation.

It is essential for institutions and political actors to recognize that the process of constructing solutions to structural problems in the country must necessarily involve the Council. Its legitimacy needs to be established and depends on the strength and political interest vested in it, as well as the results it will be able to deliver.

Some challenges immediately present themselves. The first is the establishment of an institutional identity. This identity entails recognizing the importance and legitimacy of the "other." In other words, Council members need to demonstrate empathy and understand the need for a holistic view of the federation. This perspective should encompass the mutual interests of the various levels of government and extend beyond the tradition of solely vocalizing demands to the federal government as the ultimate problem solver. Dialogue, facilitated by the establishment of the federative table, is already an important catalyst for this process.

Another challenge is defining the agenda. The prospect of debating and seeking structuring agendas for the federation needs to be linked to conjunctural challenges. Conjunctural and urgent problems must be addressed by the Council of the Federation, which, however, cannot refrain from seeking the necessary consensus around structuring solutions. In short, the fundamental challenge for the Council is to seek structural solutions to conjunctural problems. Otherwise, it may start to act as a conciliation chamber or a service counter for specific demands - functions already performed by other institutions in the Brazilian federation.

The construction of the institutional place of the Council, regarding its relationship with sectoral governance structures — such as the Tripartite Health Intermanagers Commission —, also needs to be clarified. When and which topics will be the subject of deliberation within the Council in the case where the public policy sector already has its own intergovernmental council? How will the Council of the Federation operate alongside sectors that do not yet have such structures? These are open questions. Nevertheless, the Council presents itself as a privileged place to look at and debate the problems of the federation from a holistic and cross-sectoral perspective. Not to mention the political strength that its deliberations can obtain, even influencing the agendas of the judiciary and the legislature.

Another challenge lies in the different stages of institutional maturity of the consortia and entities that make up the Council. Some of them still lack technical-administrative structure, while others have a large technical support staff. Moreover, not all of them had the institutional prerogative of representing the interests of their members. This is the case for some consortia, which emerged to instrumentalize the implementation of public policies, for example.

These are some of the most apparent obstacles, but only the functioning of the Council and the ability of political actors who lead it to conduct and articulate can contribute to overcoming them. The fact is that the success of the Council of the Federation in deepening intergovernmental cooperation and improving policies and institutional reforms depends on building a new federative political culture. A culture that the Council of the Federation itself will have to cultivate.

References

Agranoff, R. (2012). *Collaborating to manage: A primer for the public sector*. Washington, DC: Georgetown University Press.

Arretche, M. T. S. (1999). Políticas sociais no Brasil: Descentralização em um Estado federativo. *Revista Brasileira de Ciências Sociais, 14*(10), 111-140.

Arretche, M. (2012). *Democracia, federalismo e centralização no Brasil*. Rio de Janeiro: Editora FGV.

Abrúcio, F. L. (2005). A coordenação federativa no Brasil: A experiência do período FHC e os desafios do governo Lula. *Revista de Sociologia e Política, 24*, 41-67.

Abrucio, F. L., Grin, E. J., Franzese, C., Segatto, C. I., & Couto, C. G. (2020). Combate à COVID-19 sob o federalismo bolsonarista: Um caso de descoordenação intergovernamental. *Revista de Administração Pública, 54*(4), 663-677.

Carvalho, J. M. de. (1987). *Os bestializados: O Rio de Janeiro e a República que não foi*. São Paulo: Companhia das Letras.

Franzese, C. (2010). *Federalismo cooperativo no Brasil: Da Constituição de 1988 à constituição dos sistemas de políticas públicas*. Rio de Janeiro: FGV EAESP.

Gomide, A. de Á., Sá e Silva, M. M., & Leopoldi, M. A. (2023). Políticas públicas em contexto de retrocesso democrático e populismo reacionário: Desmontes e reconfigurações. In: A. A. Gomide, M.M. Sá e Silva, and M. A. Leopoldi (Eds.). *Desmonte e reconfiguração de políticas públicas (2016-2022)* (pp. 13-42). Rio de Janeiro: Ipea; INCT/PPED.

Gomes, S., Silva, A. L. N., Segatto, C. I., & Santos, A. (2022). A atuação coordenadora do governo do Rio Grande do Norte no combate à covid-19: Inovação em tempos de crise? *Saúde e Sociedade, 31*(4), 1-13.

Grin, E. J., & Abrucio, F. L. (2018). O comitê e articulação federativa no governo Lula: Os percalços da cooperação territorial. *Revista Brasileira de Ciências Sociais, 33*(97), e339703.

Palotti, P., & Machado, J. A. (2014). Coordenação federativa e a "armadilha da decisão conjunta": As comissões de articulação intergovernamental das políticas sociais no Brasil. *Dados – Revista de Ciências Sociais, 57*(2), 399-441.

Palotti, P., Filgueiras, F., & Testa, G. G. (2023). Desmobilização institucional e estilos de governança multinível: O caso da CIT da saúde no governo federal brasileiro na pandemia de Covid-19. In: A. A. Gomide, M.M. Sá e Silva, and M. A. Leopoldi (Eds.) *Desmonte e reconfiguração de políticas públicas (2016-2022)* (pp. 529-555). Rio de Janeiro: IPEA; INCT/PPED.

Paiva, A. B. de et al. (2023). Assistência social. *Políticas sociais: Acompanhamento e análise, 30*, 1-55. Brasília: Ipea.

Palotti, P., Lício, E. C., Gomes, S., Segatto, C. I., & Silva, A. L. N. (Eds.). (2023). *E os estados? Federalismo, relações intergovernamentais e políticas públicas no Brasil contemporâneo*. Rio de Janeiro: Ipea.

Silva, A. L. N., Segatto, C. I., Palotti, P., Lício, E. C., & Gomes, S. (2023). Os estados nas diferentes agendas de pesquisa e panorama geral dos achados no livro. In P. Palotti, E. C. Lício, S. Gomes, C. I. Segatto, & A. L. N. Silva (Eds.), *E os Estados? Federalismo, relações intergovernamentais e políticas públicas no Brasil contemporâneo* (pp. 17-42). Rio de Janeiro: Ipea.

THE ROLE OF SECOND CHAMBERS IN FEDERATIONS: A COMPARATIVE APPROACH

Antonios Souris

Introduction

This chapter deals with second chambers in federal systems from a comparative perspective. Second chambers best capture the idea of shared rule inherent to federal systems, since they ensure that the constituent units (i.e., states, provinces, *Länder*) are represented and participate in federal decision-making. Therefore, second chambers are at the centre of federal politics. Unsurprisingly, they have also attracted a great deal of scholarly interest (Gamper, 2018; Mueller, Vatter, & Dick, 2023; Russell, 2001; Watts, 2010; Noël, 2022). After a brief discussion of bicameralism and federalism, the chapter examines the institutional design of second chambers, focusing on three core elements: the selection of their members, the representation of the constituent units in their composition, and their powers in law-making. In the chapter, I advance two arguments: firstly, the institutional propositions of federal second chambers reveal that there is no single model but a large variety of institutional designs around the world. Secondly – and other than often claimed –, second chambers are, in principle, no barrier to federal democracy. On the contrary, they are a vital part of it – at least if the political actors comply with the "rules of the game". Finally, the chapter raises several open questions for comparative federalism scholarship regarding the role of second chambers in the current era of emergencies.

Bicameralism and federalism

In the Federalist Papers, James Madison expressed his views on bicameralism in several of his writings. According to Madison, a bicameral legislature provides an effective system of checks and balances. Two separate chambers would serve as a safeguard against a potential tyranny of the majority, preventing ill-considered or even oppressive legislation (Federalist No. 10, No. 51). Madison also saw bicameralism as a means to balance the interests of the states and the people. The House of Representatives, elected directedly by the people, would ensure popular representation. On the other hand, the Senate would represent the interests of the states and, at the same time, protect the rights of the smaller states against potential domination by larger ones (Federalist No. 39).

Madison also believed that a bicameral legislature would enhance law-making. The two chambers would contribute different perspectives to policymaking, allowing for more thoughtful and comprehensive discussions. The Senate was seen as the chamber of greater stability and experience, providing a check on the passions and strategic interests that could dominate the House of Representatives. It was thus envisioned as being capable of carefully reviewing and amending legislations (Federalist No. 62).[8] The idea of the second chamber as the wiser part of parliament, counteracting the short-sightedness of politics with long-term thinking to realize better legislation, has become received wisdom (Schüttemeyer & Sturm, 1992, p. 519). In Germany, for example, the *Bundesrat* is praised in a similar manner (Hoffmann & Wisser, 2012).

Institutional design

Institutions are never designed in an empty space. In Brazil, the first republican constitution of 1891 took the U.S. Senate as the model for the design of the *Senado Federal*. The South African National Council of Provinces resembles several ideas of the German *Bundesrat*. One reason for this is that South African lawmakers were advised by German experts during the constitutional reform in the 1990s (Nolting, 2010, pp. 148–49). Moreover, institutional design can be dependent on historical factors, creating path dependencies. For example, the founders of the German constitution (Basic Law) discussed the model of a Senate after the Second World War. However, they eventually decided to establish the *Bundesrat*, building on the institutional design that was envisioned a century earlier.

---

[8] Allegedly, in a conversation with George Washington, Thomas Jefferson once compared the role of the Senate in politics with hot tea. Hot tea only becomes drinkable if poured from the cup into the saucer and back (Schüttemeyer & Sturm, 1992, p. 519).

The constitution of the "North German Federation", adopted in 1867, already designed a *Bundesrat* that consisted of delegates appointed by the state governments.

As a result, there is a large variation in institutional design. This chapter focuses on three core elements of institutional design: the selection of the members, the representation of constituent units, and powers in law-making.

Selection of the members

Regarding the methods of selection for members of federal second chambers, there are four groups. Firstly, there are second chambers which are directly elected, following the U.S. model. This group also includes Argentina, Brazil, Mexico, Australia, or Nigeria (Noël, 2022, pp. 15-16). Secondly, there are indirectly elected second chambers. In Austria, the members of the *Bundesrat* are elected by the state parliaments (Constitution of Austria, article 35). The third mode of selection is appointment. This group includes Canada, where senators are appointed by the governor-general on behalf of the prime minister as the head of the federal government (Noël, 2022, p. 17). In Germany, the *Bundesrat* is made-up of delegates appointed by the state governments (Basic Law, article 51). These delegates are usually cabinet members of the state governments as well as civil servants who act as deputy members in the *Bundesrat* committees (Finke et al., 2020). Finally, there are mixed memberships. The South African National Council of Provinces somewhat combines the two modes of selection we find in Austria and in Germany. The National Council has 90 seats (ten seats per province): 54 delegates are selected by the provincial legislatures and 36 delegates are appointed by the provincial government (Constitution of South Africa, articles 60, 61).

Representation of constituent units

There is, firstly, equal representation of the constituent units. Most prominently, the U.S. Senate has two senators per state. Following the U.S. model, there are three senators per constituent unit in the Brazilian *Senado Federal* and the Argentinian *Senado de la Nación*. Other federations favour a system of weighted representation. In Germany, for example, the constitution defines four groups of constituent units (*Länder*) in terms of their population. Depending on the population size, the state governments have between three and six votes in the *Bundesrat* (Basic Law, article 51). The smallest Land, Bremen (around 600.000 inhabitants) has three votes, and the largest one, North Rhine-Westphalia (around 18 million inhabitants) has six votes. Weighted regional representation can help protecting minority rights or special interests. This is, for example, the case in Belgium. Regional representation in the Belgian Senate is designed to ensure a balance between the linguistic communities and regions of the country. For some important issues, the constitution requires majorities within both the French speaking and the Dutch speaking members in the Senate (Constitution of Belgium, article 43). In India, not only the constituent units are represented in the second chamber. The President also appoints twelve members to the *Rajya Sabha* with proven knowledge or experience in literature, science, art, or social service (Constitution of India, article 80).

Powers

The most important function of second chambers is to represent the constituent units' concerns in federal law-making. Their role in this arises not only from their involvement in the legislative process, but from their veto powers towards the first chamber in particular. On the one hand, there are federations, such as the U.S. and Australia, in which second chambers usually have an absolute veto. However, there are stark differences in conflict resolution. The U.S. Congress heavily relies on mediation committees between the House of Representatives and the Senate. In Australia, the Senate's absolute veto power comes along with a double dissolution procedure and joint sitting – which rarely takes place though. On the other hand, in Argentina and India, the *Senado de la Nación* and the *Rajya Sabha* generally have a suspensive veto only. There is a third group of federations where the veto power of the second chamber depends on the issue at stake. This group includes Austria, Germany, and South Africa. In Austria, the *Bundesrat* has an absolute veto on constitutional amendments bills affecting the constituent units (*Länder*), and on the approval of international treaties affecting their responsibilities. Regarding ordinary bills, the Austrian *Bundesrat* only has a suspensive veto (which can be overridden by a simple majority in the first chamber), while it does not deal with budget bills at all. In South Africa, the veto power also varies with type of legislation. Like in Austria, the National Council of Provinces has an absolute veto on constitutional amendment bills which affect the responsibilities, institutions, or boundaries of provinces. The National Council has no veto power on constitutional amendment bills that do not affect the provinces, while it has is a suspensive veto on legislative bills which do affect them. These bills can be overridden by a qualified majority of two-thirds in the first chamber. Regarding legislative bills that do not affect provinces and budget bills, the first chamber can override the National Council's suspensive veto through a simple majority vote (Noël, 2022, p. 43-48).

Beyond law-making, there are additional functions. Second chambers have appointment powers. For example, the German *Bundesrat* elects half of the judges of the constitutional court (Basic Law, article 94). In the U.S., Argentina, and Brazil, second chambers participate in impeachment procedures against the president (Noël, 2022, pp. 28-29). The idea is that power is institutionally distributed in such a way that impeachment cannot be easily exploited by political factions. The second chamber plays a key role in this regard. In the U.S., impeachment proceedings foresee that the House of Representatives charges an official of the federal government by approving articles of impeachment by a simple majority vote (U.S. Constitution, article 1, section 2). These articles are sent to the Senate, which then sits as a "High Court of Impeachment". It considers evidence, hears witnesses, and eventually vote to acquit or convict the impeached official. The U.S. Constitution (article 1, section 3) requires a two-thirds vote of the Senate to convict the impeached official.[9]

In many federations, second chambers also play an important role in states of exception in times of emergency (Noël, 2022, pp. 28-29). In Argentina, the Senate must authorize the President to declare a state of siege one or several places of the Republic in case of a foreign attack (Constitution of Argentina, article 61). In the event of an internal state of emergency, the German *Bundesrat* can demand from the federal government to end the deployment of police forces (Basic Law, article 91). In the event of an external state of emergency, a "state of defense" (*Verteidigungsfall*) can only be declared with the consent of the *Bundesrat*. Moreover, it can request the first chamber (*Bundestag*) to decide on the termination of the "state of defense" and can declare it terminated together with the *Bundestag* (Basic Law, article 115a). If the *Bundestag* is no longer able to convene, the so-called

---

[9] The second impeachment procedure against U.S.-President Donald Trump that followed the events leading to the attack of Capitol Hill has highlighted how high this hurdle is. Despite seven Republican senators voting in favor of conviction, it ultimately failed as the two-thirds majority was not reached.

"Joint Committee" (*Gemeinsamer Ausschuss*) is formed to act in place of *Bundestag* and *Bundesrat*. Sixteen of the 48 members of this committee are delegates of the *Bundesrat*. The Joint Committee exercises the rights of both chambers during the "state of defense" (Basic Law, article 115a and 115e).

Second chambers and federal democracy

Second chambers are often criticized for violating democratic principles. According to Watts (2010), this criticism relates to one's specific understanding of democracy. Some highlight its majoritarian essence, i.e., the rule by the *demos*. Most federations have established second chambers which favor the smaller constituent units. Therefore, the cardinal principle of democracy – that is, one person, one vote – would be violated. In the German *Bundesrat*, a single vote of Bremen counts significantly more than one in North Rhine-Westphalia. In the U.S. Senate, a single vote of Wyoming, the least populated state, counts around 70 times more than in the one of California, the most populous state. Watts (2010, pp. 43-45) argues that this narrow focus on majoritarian democratic principles can be misleading and suggests a different interpretation based on a broader understanding of liberal democracy. Second chambers do not constrain the *demos* but have, in fact, *demos*-enabling effects. They create another opportunity for citizens' preferences to be achieved. At the same time, they are an expression of the fact that federations recognize the distinct *demoi* in their constituent units. Moreover, second chambers are a manifestation of the checks and balances inherent to modern liberal democracies and help protecting minority rights. Therefore, they play a crucial role in integrating different societal groups, creating compromises and consensus, and thus in keeping the federation together.

Without the politics, there is no full picture of the role second chambers play in federal democracies, however. The behavior of political parties is particularly important in this regard. Parties are the main actors in second chambers, determining how theoretic ideas or formal procedures come to life. In other words, ideas and procedures can be understood as the "rules of the game" and parties as the players. Just like in sports, political players regularly test the limits and functionality of the rules of the game. Many federations have experienced how party politics and growing political polarization can negatively affect the functioning of legislatures. In the U.S. senate, for example, conflicts along party lines occurs much more frequent (Curry &

Lee, 2020, p. 4), which, depending on the majority constellation, makes gridlock more likely. The dominance of party politics goes against the idea of a second chamber that ensures territorial representation and deliberation towards the superior legislative outcome as envisioned by Madison.

However, there are also examples of second chambers that function exactly as intended. One of these examples is the German *Bundesrat*. Based on a dataset which includes more than 51.000 decisions in its committees between 1991 and 2013, Finke et al. (2020) find that territorial and institutional interests did not fall victim to party competition. The data show that territorial interests of the state representatives prevailed, while also institutional interests played an important role. These interests primarily refer to administrative concerns of the *Länder* ministries and bureaucracies regarding policies. In Germany, most legislation is made at the national level. The *Länder* must administer and implement the legislation. Therefore, the knowledge and experience are located rather at the subnational level. Through the *Bundesrat*, the *Länder* representatives feed this expertise into national policymaking. Around 12 percent of the decisions were subject to party competition, ranking way below territorial and institutional interests. Hence, party politics in the *Bundesrat* does not impair the functioning of the German political system. This result is also confirmed by another figure: gridlock in the *Bundesrat* is well documented, namely as failed bills of the federal government or the *Bundestag*, which account for a relatively small proportion of all bills – normally a handful per federal legislative period of four years (Müller et al., 2020, pp. 26-31). In the last legislative period of the *Bundestag* (2017-2021), only four bills were blocked by the *Bundesrat* (Bundesrat, 2021).

Unlike in the U.S., the multi-party system in Germany with different governing coalitions at both federal levels thwarts a clear-cut confrontation between one *Bundestag* majority on the one hand and one *Bundesrat* majority on the other hand. Beyond coalition politics, the German political system creates further incentives for parties to cooperate. Party leaders at both levels of government must collaborate and find joint solutions both within the vertically integrated party organizations as well as in a plethora of intergovernmental fora. These cooperative structures tend to counteract confrontational political behavior (Souris, Kropp, & Nguyen, 2023). In the *Bundesrat*, the data show that parties do not negotiate based on zero-sum games. Instead, they aim at achieving political compromises (Müller et al., 2020, p. 28).

Reflections and open questions

There are at least three questions regarding second chambers that need further comparative assessment. Firstly, are there better or worse institutional models of second chambers, and what do we mean by the terms "better" or "worse" in this regard? The answers to these questions clearly depend on what function the second chamber is expected to fulfil in a political system. Moreover, "better" or "worse" performances of political institutions are always a snapshot in time. The U.S. Senate has been heavily affected by the growing polarization in American society and politics. On the other hand, the data on decision-making in the German *Bundesrat* suggests that it has been less captured by party politics. However, just because it has not happened yet does not mean it never will. The *Bundesrat* consists of members of the state governments. The far-right "Alternative for Germany" (AfD) is currently, in the beginning of the 2020s, in the opposition only and thus not represented in the *Bundesrat*. Once this situation changes – the AfD is gaining public support in light of the multiple crises Germany experiences –, a similar trend towards partisan-motivated gridlock is at least conceivable.

Secondly, what is meant by "territorial interests", and what are, by contrast, "party interests"? This is a crucial distinction when it comes to second chambers because territorial interests are widely perceived as being more legitimate than party interests. In Germany, a veto by the *Bundesrat* would be perceived differently (more legitimate) if it is orchestrated by the *Länder* vis-à-vis the federal government than if it were due to party strategies and conflict (less legitimate). There is a similar view in other federal democracies. In times of crisis, in particular such as the COVID-19 pandemic, political decisions must be perceived as legitimate in order not to lose public support (Guderjan, Kölling, & Schnabel, 2023). Beyond single case studies, it would be thus an important task for scholars of comparative federalism to examine the territorial and partisan dimension of decision-making in second chambers and the actual effects on public support of policies.

Finally, how do second chambers respond to the new challenges in an era of emergencies and how can they contribute to solving the multiple crises federal democracies experience? According to Madison, second chambers have the responsibility to enhance legislation and get the heat out of politics. However, do we have the time that the wise (wo)man – to stay with Madison's original image of the U.S. Senate – sit together and deliberate about policy? How can second chambers adjust to the new short-termism of politics, or should they counteract it? Do federal democracies need this kind of institution exactly in this era of emergencies and the democratic backlash that comes along with it? Finding reliable answers to these questions is only possible by comparing and learning from the different cases and experiences of federal democracies around the world.

References

Bundesrat (2021, November 8). *Statistik Der Parlamentarischen Arbeit Des Bundesrates*. Retrieved March 25, 2024, from https://www.bundesrat.de/SharedDocs/downloads/DE/statistik/19wp.pdf;jsessionid=72CEF028646452DBC12370F40F93A6D2.live531?__blob=publicationFile&v=53

Curry, J. M., & F. E. Lee (2020). *The Limits of Party: Congress and Lawmaking in a Polarized Era*. The University of Chicago Press. Retrieved from https://doi.10.7208/chicago/9780226716497.001.0001

Finke, P., Müller, M. M., Souris, A., & Sturm, R. (2020). Representation of Partisan, Territorial, and Institutional Interests in Second Chambers: Evidence from the German Bundesrat and Its Committees. *Publius: The Journal of Federalism, 50*(2), 213-236.

Gamper, A. (2018). Legislative Functions of Second Chambers in Federal Systems. *Perspectives on Federalism, 10*(2), 117-133.

Guderjan, M., Kölling, M., & Schnabel, J. (2023). Multilevel Crisis Management: COVID-19 Responses in Federal and Decentralised Polities. In Europäisches Zentrum für Föderalismus-Forschung Tübingen (EZFF). *Jahrbuch Des Föderalismus 2023* (pp. 178-192). Nomos Verlagsgesellschaft mbH & Co. KG.

Hoffmann, J., & Wisser, M. (2012). Sachverständige Rechtsetzung: Die Ausschüsse des Bundesrates in der Gesetzgebung des Bundes. *Zeitschrift für Parlamentsfragen, 43*(3), 598-608.

Mueller, S., Vatter, A., & Dick, S. (2023). A New Index of Bicameralism: Taking Legitimacy Seriously. *The Journal of Legislative Studies, 29*(2), 312-336.

Müller, M. M., Sturm, R., Finke, P., & Souris, A. (2020). *Parteipolitik im Bundesrat: Der Bundesrat und seine Ausschüsse*. Nomos Verlagsgesellschaft mbH & Co. KG.

Noël, T. (2022). *Second Chambers in Federal Systems*. International Institute for Democracy and Electoral Assistance (International IDEA). Retrieved from https://doi.org/10.31752/idea.2022.63

Nolting, A. K. (2010). Südafrika: Der Nationalrat Der Provinzen. In G. Riescher, S. Ruß, & C. M. Haas, *Zweite Kammern* (pp. 145–64). Oldenbourg.

Russell, M. (2001). What Are Second Chambers For? *Parliamentary Affairs, 54*(3), 442-458.

Schüttemeyer, S., & Sturm, R. (1992). Wozu Zweite Kammern? Zur Repräsentation und Funktionalität Zweiter Kammern in westlichen Demokratien. *Zeitschrift fur Parlamentsfragen, 23*(3), 517-536.

Souris, A., Kropp, S., & Nguyen, C. (2023). Attributing Blame: How Political Parties in Germany Leverage Cooperative Federalism. *West European Politics*, 1-27.

Watts, R. (2010). Federal Second Chambers Compared. In R. Hrbek (Ed.), *Legislatures in Federal Systems and Multi-Level Governance* (pp. 31–46). Nomos Verlagsgesellschaft mbH & Co. KG.

THE ROLE OF UPPER HOUSES IN FEDERATIONS: THE BRAZILIAN PERSPECTIVE

Cláudio Gonçalves Couto

Introduction

I will present a Brazilian perspective on our upper house, or more precisely, on the characteristics of the Brazilian bicameral system. In Brazil, rather than being a federative chamber or the "house of the states" like in other federative countries, the Federal Senate functions as a revising chamber of the Chamber of Deputies' decisions.

This is not due to a deviation from its institutional purposes, but because the Senate was originally created with such a political function. Partly, this relates to the historical origins of the Senate in Brazil, which date back to the monarchical period (1822-1889) when the country was unitary. Brazil only became a federation in 1889, at the same time it was transformed into a republic and a presidential system. There is a path-dependency between the original institutional role of the Upper House in Brazil and its continuous operation throughout history.

The second reason for this functioning of the Brazilian Senate in this manner is the operation of the multiparty congressional system and its interaction with the Executive Branch. Brazil has what is called "coalition presidentialism", which requires the head of government to frame and coordinate multi-party coalitions in Congress, both in the Federal Senate and in the Chamber of Deputies. Hence, the dynamics of the relationship between the two powers shape the internal functioning of the two houses of Congress in a similar way.

What kind of bicameralism?

Brazil has some specificities that must be considered. The first one has to do with the reasons for the existence of a bicameral system in Brazil. Before becoming a Federal Republic, it was a unitary monarchy during the 19th century. So, we must consider how the Senate and the House were created at that time.

They were not created to solve federative problems, since this was a unitary country, but to deal with another kind of issues. Our bicameralism was not exactly something designed to create a system of checks and balances, but much more, at that time, it was created to provide a mixed government. In the same terms that we have mixed governments elsewhere, considering two different groups in society, the nobles, and the rest of the plebeian part of the society. So, some characteristics here are specifically important. First, the position of senator at that time was for life and the senators were appointed by the emperor after being elected indirectly at the provincial level.

Then we had two different kinds of voters: the parish voters who voted for provincial voters, and the provincial voters who were responsible for electing not only the senators but also the deputies. Hence, it was an indirect form of election.

Besides that, the deputies were not elected for life, but for some years, differently from the senators. Then, the Senate in Brazil at that time was a kind of aristocratic chamber, a house of lords. This is why it had much more to do with a mixed government than exactly with a system of checks and balances.

Additionally, every province would not be represented by the same number or an equal number of senators considering their population. Actually, both the deputies and the senators were calculated in what regard their numbers in terms of representation based on the size of the population of each province. We had a smaller number of senators than of deputies. The number of senators was defined considering the number of deputies per province, and after that, both houses were formed considering the distribution of population throughout the whole country.

Finally, the senators were supposed to be the oldest and wisest among the members of parliament – at that time at least 40 years old – but also the princes of the Brazilian empire were native members of the Senate. These are the origins of Brazilian bicameralism.

Such an origin created a path dependence to the framing of the Republic, inaugurated in 1889, when Brazil was also transformed into a federation. There was a considerable degree of survival of features present at the original model of bicameralism framed during the monarchic period.

Brazil emulated the American model in terms of the design of its political system: federalism, presidential government and – what specially matters for this discussion – bicameralism. But it was not a perfect copy in what regards the functioning of both houses of Congress, at least in terms of the theory underpinning the creation of bicameral systems in federal and republican countries like Brazil or the United States.

Brazil has a Senate that used to work much more as a partisan house than properly as a federal house [see more about that in the chapter by Antonios Souris in this volume]. That is, the Senate in Brazil is not the House of the states; it is the second House of the parties. This is what must be considered since the beginning of the bicameral system in Brazil during the Republic.

More than anything, it is a revising chamber that has to reconsider what comes from the House. Additionally, we must consider that historically, the executive branch in Brazil has played a prominent role in proposing legislation. Since the beginning of the Republic in the late 19th century, all bills originating from the executive branch have initially been subject to deliberation in the House, not in the Senate. This is significant because the chamber where the legislation begins its analysis is the one that ultimately determines what will be transformed into law.

To provide an example, if a bill is proposed by the executive branch, it goes to the House, where it may be amended. Then, it proceeds to the Senate, where further amendments may occur. However, if the House chooses not to accept the Senate's amendments and instead passes the bill as initially established, this version prevails. Consequently, deputies have an advantage over senators concerning a significant portion of the legislation, particularly legislation proposed by the executive branch. While similar dynamics occur with legislation proposed by deputies and senators themselves, the predominance of the executive branch, especially since the end of the military dictatorship, has further emphasized the prominence of the House over the Senate in the legislative process.

As a point of interest, one of Brazil's oldest newspapers, *O Estado de São Paulo*, was established in the 1870s under the name *Province of São Paulo*. When the Republic was established, the transition to a federal system led to the newspaper's renaming as *The State of São Paulo*. Despite the name change, it remains the same newspaper and serves as a significant representative of the *Paulista* soul and identity. This transition in names exemplifies the continuity I am emphasizing here. That is, names change, but the essence of things often remains constant.

In the Senate, certain responsibilities of senators extend beyond federal issues. For instance, they have the authority to judge the president and certain high officials, such as members of the Supreme Court, for crimes or misconduct. This role was established with the founding of the Brazilian Republic and Federation in 1889 and remains unchanged. However, its relevance to federative issues is less direct. Instead, it reflects the Senate's composition of experienced and influential politicians, akin to *caciques* or bosses. The Senate comprises the political elite of different states, who consequently hold national political influence. In contrast, the lower house primarily consists of more ordinary politicians.

Another point of interest is that while the House is very powerful in terms of considering legislation as a whole, especially the bills proposed by the executive branch, the Senate houses political party leaders. Thus, we observe a distinction between the types of politicians present in each chamber, with the Senate representing a somewhat aristocratic assembly. Despite the absence of an aristocratic system in the Republic, the Senate maintains a crucial role. Responsibilities such as approving nominations, appointments to the Supreme Court or to the Court of Audits, and ambassadors for foreign service is a special duty for the Senate, but certainly it is not exactly a federative one. Therefore, while the Senate serves as an upper house, it cannot be strictly labeled as the chamber of the states.

How can we measure that? There are studies, mentioned at the references of this chapter, that consider the alignment of roll call votes both for deputies and for senators. What these studies show is that, in both cases, both in the Senate and in the House, we find a very similar and partisan behavior. In the Brazilian coalition presidential system, we have these kinds of coalitions framed by the executive branch to govern, working in both the Senate and the House, resulting in a repetition of the pattern in both chambers. It is not a complete repetition because, besides that, we have a somewhat symmetric case of bicameralism; we do not have congruent bicameralism. The way of electing deputies for the House and senators for the Federal Senate is different.

There is a proportional representative system to elect deputies, and a majoritarian system of vote for senators. In the case of proportional representation for deputies, it is an open list, so one can vote for individual candidates nominally. In the case of the Senate, it is only a nominal vote for the candidate, but it follows a first-past-the-post system, creating different combinations of partisan representation either in the Senate or in the House. Such electoral outcomes affect policymaking and the political dynamics between the two branches of government because the executive may have to build somewhat different party coalitions either the Senate or the House due to different sizes of parties in each chamber, what makes a difference

Because of these partisan differences between both chambers, sometimes the Senate plays a moderating role, but not always. It is possible to exist different partisan compositions in both houses, somewhat like in the US when there is a case of divided government. However, whereas in the United States there is a bipartisan system allowing for two different combinations of the majority in both the House and the Senate, in Brazil we have a very fragmented multiparty system, providing for different kaleidoscopes of parties in the House and the Senate.

This does not mean that senators never work in a state-oriented manner. It can happen, but only when very specific issues related to state interests are at stake. A historical and significant example occurred in 2012 when discussing the distribution of oil royalties from the exploitation of oil in the Brazilian shore. In states like Rio de Janeiro or Espírito Santo, a considerable amount of revenue came from oil royalties due to oil exploitation on their coasts. At that time, there was a redefinition of the sharing of revenues, considering that everything from the soil belongs to the Union, and thus the revenues should be shared more equally. Consequently, states like Rio de Janeiro and Espírito Santo would lose a lot of money, affecting not only how senators voted but also deputies; they voted in a state-oriented manner. It would have been a political suicide for a deputy from Rio de Janeiro, for example, to vote in favor of this new distribution. But again, the behavior was the same both in the House and the Senate.

And, besides that, another point must be stressed. On one hand, we have equal representation for the states in the Brazilian Senate; however, we do not have an exact proportional representation for deputies in the House. Why is that? Well, the current Brazilian Constitution and former constitutions (there have been seven constitutions in Brazil since the empire) establish that the representation of states in the House should not be strictly proportional. The Brazilian Constitution of 1988 provides that the minimum number of deputies that a state must have in the House is 8, and the maximum is 70. So, what happens? Some underpopulated members of the federation are overrepresented (such as some states in the northern and Amazon regions), whereas larger states are underrepresented (especially São Paulo). According to the latest census numbers, São Paulo should have 115 deputies if we had a one-citizen-one-vote system, but it has only 70. On the other hand, the state of Roraima, in the north, should have just one deputy (because it is impossible to have fewer than one), but it has 8.

There are some other cases like these, which create an imbalance of representation not only in the Senate, establishing a system of equal representation between states, or somewhat like in Germany and some other federations, where you do not have exactly equal representation per state but a more balanced representation of federal unities in the so-called Federative House.

In Brazil we have this situation of over-representation of the smaller states in both houses of Congress, thereby duplicating the strengthening of smaller states' congressional representation. What kind of bicameralism is this? It is not exactly a federative bicameralism. It is a system that tries to create some checks and balances between both houses. It really works and it was quite important, for example, during Bolsonaro's administration, where the Senate was a hindrance to very radical policies proposed by the President and endorsed by the Chamber of Deputies. They were blocked in the Senate. So, it made a difference, but not in a federative manner.

Final remarks

As we can see, when talking about the Brazilian bicameral system, we talk much more about coalition presidentialism than federalism. And this happens despite a widespread belief, even in Brazil, that the Senate is the "house of the states". It is not, at least no more than the Chamber of Deputies. Perhaps that is why, at the same time that we call the Upper House the "Federal Senate", we also call the members of the Lower House "Federal Deputies". None of them is especially federal, except on very special occasions, when both chambers (and their members) work on a federal (or state) basis.

References

Araújo, P. M. (2009). *O Bicameralismo no Brasil: as bases institucionais e políticas do desempenho legislativo do Senado Federal (1989-2004)* [Doctoral dissertation, UFMG]. Retrieved from https://repositorio.ufmg.br/handle/1843/BUBD-89HJ9T

Araújo, P. M. (2012). O bicameralismo no Brasil: argumentos sobre a importância do Senado na análise do processo decisório federal. *Política & Sociedade, 11*(21), 83.

Arretche, M. (2013). Quando instituições federativas fortalecem o governo central?. *Novos Estudos - CEBRAP, 95*, 39-57.

Lemos, L. B., & Llanos, M. (2007). O Senado e as aprovações de autoridades: um estudo comparativo entre Argentina e Brasil. *Revista Brasileira de Ciências Sociais, 22*, 115-138.

Neiva, P., & Soares, M. (2013). Senado brasileiro: casa federativa ou partidária?. *Revista Brasileira de Ciências Sociais, 28*(81), 97-115.

Neiva, P. (2011). Coesão e Disciplina Partidária no Senado Federal. *DADOS – Revista de Ciências Sociais, 54*(2), 289-318.

Ricci, P. (2008). A produção legislativa de iniciativa parlamentar no Congresso Brasileiro: diferenças e similaridades entre a Câmara dos Deputados e o Senado Federal. In L. B. Lemos (Ed.), *O Senado Federal Brasileiro no Pós-Constituinte* (pp. 237-271). Brasília: Unilegis; Senado Federal

Silva, R. S. (2010). *Senado: Casa de Senhores? Os perfis de carreira dos senadores eleitos entre 1990 e 2006* [Master dissertation, UFRGS]. Retrieved from https://lume.ufrgs.br/handle/10183/27956

ABOUT THE EDITORS

Eduardo Grin is PhD in Public Administration and Government, Professor and Researcher at Fundação Getulio Vargas/São Paulo where he teaches on local government, decentralization, federalism, intergovernmental relations, and public policies. He was Visiting scholar at University of Berkley. He is professor at University of Valle (Colombia). He has published books and articles on Brazilian and Latin American federations in *Public Administration Review*, *Urban Affairs Review*, *Public Organization Review*, among others.

Orcid: 0000-0002-0488-8487

Rogerio Schlegel is an associate professor at the Federal University of São Paulo (UNIFESP) with a PhD in Political Science (Universidade de São Paulo). He has published in international journals such as *Publius: The Journal of Federalism*, *Regional & Federal Studies*, *Journal of Politics in Latin America*, and *Brazilian Political Science Review*. He was a visiting scholar at Columbia University (2018-2019) and the University of Cambridge (2012-2013), a junior visiting scholar at the University of Oxford (2008-2009) and recently participated in the comparative project Why De/Centralization in Federations. His research interests include Federalism, Public Policy, Education, and Media Studies.

Orcid: 0000-0002-1297-0819

Johanna Schnabel is a Lecturer at the Chair of German Politics, Otto Suhr Institute of Political Science, Freie Universität Berlin. She holds a PhD in Political Science from the University of Lausanne, Switzerland and was a postdoctoral researcher at the University of Kent, United Kingdom. Her research largely focuses on intergovernmental relations and public policy in federal and decentralized countries. She has published widely on the management of fiscal and public health crises and the coordination of public policymaking. She is the author of *Managing Interdependencies in Federal Systems. Intergovernmental Councils and the Making of Public Policy* (Palgrave, 2020). Her research has also been published in *Publius: The Journal of Federalism*, *Regional & Federal Studies*, and *West European Politics*, among others.

Orcid: 0000-0002-6160-1083

ABOUT THE ASSISTANT EDITOR

Camila Nastari Fernandes is a postdoctoral researcher in Social Sciences at the Federal University of São Paulo (UNIFESP), currently working on responsible innovation in social policies. She received her Ph.D. (2022) and Master's (2013) degrees in Territorial Planning and Management from the Federal University of ABC (UFABC), working on the topic of institutions in urban policies. She completed a postdoctoral fellowship as a visiting researcher at the École de Santé Publique de l'Université de Montréal (UdeM). Her research interests include Public policy, Institutions, Governance and Urban Studies.

Orcid: 0000-0002-4430-604X

ABOUT THE AUTHORS

Alan Fenna, BA (Alberta), MA (Queen's), PhD (York), is Professor of Politics at Curtin University, Western Australia. His most recent books, co-authored or co-edited, are *Climate Governance and Federalism* (2023); *The Constitution of Western Australia: an exploration* (2023); *Interrogating Public Policy Theory* (2019); and *Comparative Federalism: a systematic inquiry* (2015). He served as President of the Australian Political Studies Association 2009–10 and as an elected member of local government.

Orcid: 0000-0002-3692-7954

André Luis Nogueira da Silva works as Special Advisor from the Council of the Federation at the Federative Republic of Brazil. He holds a Ph.D. in Public Administration and Government from the Getulio Vargas Foundation. He is one of the editors of the book *And the States? Federalism, intergovernmental relations, and public policies in contemporary Brazil*, edited by IPEA and published in June 2023.

Orcid: 0000-0002-0934-5350

Antonios Souris is a Postdoctoral Researcher at Freie Universität Berlin. In his dissertation, he investigated policy coordination in European affairs within Germany's federal system. The dissertation received the "Federalism and Regional Studies Award" of the Institute for Federalism (Austria). His research focuses on federalism, parliaments, and the policy areas of transport and housing. It has been published in *West European Politics*, *Publius*, and *German Politics*.

Orcid: 0000-0001-7597-190X

Catarina Ianni Segatto is a Professor in the Department of Political Science at the University of São Paulo (DCP-USP) and a researcher at the Center for Metropolitan Studies (CEM). She holds a PhD in Public Administration and Government from the Sao Paulo School of Business Administration (FGV EAESP) and conducted postdoctoral research at the CEM and at the Johnson Shoyama Graduate School of Public Policy.

Orcid: 0000-0002-5094-8225

Cláudio Gonçalves Couto, political scientist, is an associate professor at Fundação Getulio Vargas in São Paulo, a productivity research fellow and member of the Political Science Advisory Committee of the National Council for Scientific and Technological Development (CNPq) and producer of the channel and podcast *Out of Politics there is No Salvation*.

Orcid: 0000-0003-0153-1877

Daniel Béland is Director of the McGill Institute for the Study of Canada and James McGill Professor in the Department of Political Science at McGill University. He has held visiting academic positions at Harvard University, the University of Bremen, the University of Nagoya, the University of Southern Denmark, and the Woodrow Wilson International Center for Scholars. Professor Béland is the Executive Editor of the *Journal of Comparative Policy Analysis* and the Editor of *Policy and Society*. A student of comparative social policy, he has published more than 20 books and 190 peer-reviewed journal articles.

Orcid: 0000-0003-2756-5629

Daniel Arias Vazquez is an associate professor at the Federal University of São Paulo (Unifesp), Department of Social Sciences, Brazil. He earned his PhD in Economic Development from University of Campinas (Unicamp), Brazil. His research areas include public policy, federalism, and government management, with a focus on the funding and evaluation of social policies. He was Academic Dean of the School of Philosophy, Letters and Human Sciences at Unifesp (2013 to 2017) and visiting scholar at the Autonomous University of Madrid, Spain (2018), with short-term research stays at the London School of Economics and Political Science, UK (2015), and at the University of Malaga, Spain (2020).

Orcid: 0000-0002-4467-3392

Elaine Cristina Lício work as Executive Secretary from the Council of the Federation at the Federative Republic of Brazil. She holds a Ph.D. in Social Policy from the University of Brasília. She is one of the editors of the book *And the States? Federalism, intergovernmental relations, and public policies in contemporary Brazil*, edited by IPEA and published in June 2023.

Orcid: 0000-0001-6829-4090

Fernando Luiz Abrucio is Professor of Public Administration and Government at the Sao Paulo School of Business Administration (FGV EAESP). He holds a PhD in Political Science at the University of São Paulo and was a visiting researcher at the Massachusetts Institute of Technology. He received the award for best young Brazilian political scientist (2001). One of his most recent books is *American Federal Systems and Covid-19* (Emerald, 2021), co-authored with B.Guy Peters and Eduardo Grin.

Orcid: 0000-0002-3883-9915

Jared Sonnicksen is professor of political science at RWTH Aachen University, Germany, responsible for the area of political systems. His areas of interest in teaching and research include: comparative government, in particular Europe and the Americas; federalism and multilevel governance in comparative perspective; as well as a cross-cutting interest in challenges of democratic governance under conditions of complexity.

Orcid: 0000-0001-7573-2722

Juan C. Olmeda is an Associate professor at El Colegio de México, in Mexico City. He holds a MA and a Phd in Political Science (Northwestern University, US) and a MA in Ethics, Politics and Public Policy (University of Essex, UK). He is the author of the book *¿La union hace la fuerza? La política de la acción colectiva de los gobernadores en Argentina, Brasil y México* (El Colegio de México 2021) and co-edited the volume *Gobernanza democrática y regionalismo en América Latina* (El Colegio de México 2022).

Orcid: 0000-0002-3696-5926

Marta Arretche is Full Professor at the Department of Political Science of the University of São Paulo and researcher of the Center for Metropolitan Studies, where she was director for 10 years. She was editor-in-chief of the Brazilian Political Science Review and vice-provost for research at the University of São Paulo. She was visiting researcher at the Department of Political Science of MIT and at the Department of Political and Social Science at the European University Institute. Her areas of research are: inequality, federalism, decentralization, social policies and welfare state.

Orcid: 0000-0002-6537-6186

Rupak Chattopadhyay has been President and CEO of the Forum of Federations since 2011. He was previously a member of the Consultative Group on the Study of Intergovernmental Relations and Dispute Resolution Mechanism, Inter-State Council, Government of India. Over the last two decades he has contributed as an expert in support of political and constitutional reforms in Ethiopia, Mexico, Myanmar, Philippines, Nepal, Sri Lanka, Tunisia and Yemen. Rupak has authored, co-authored and edited a number of books on federalism and multilevel governance.

Orcid: 0000-0003-3630-5749

Zemelak Ayitenew Ayele is a former director of, and an associate professor at the Centre for Federal and Governance Studies of Addis Ababa University. He is also an extraordinary associate professor at the Dullah Omar Institute of the University of the Western Cape. With Prof Jaap de Visser, the South African Research Chair (SARCHi) for Multilevel Government, Dr Ayele co-convenes the African School on Decentralisation (ASD). He is also currently serving as a senior political advisor at the Netherlands Institute for Multiparty Democracy (NIMD-Ethiopia). Dr Ayele received LL.B from Addis Ababa University, an Advanced Diploma in Federalism from the Institute of Federalism, Fribourg University, and LL.M and LL.D from the University of the Western Cape (UWC). He has widely published in the areas of decentralisation, federalism, and electoral democracy in Ethiopia and Africa.

Orcid: 0000-0002-1373-309X